Black Historical Figures

PROFESSIONS

Copyright © 2022 by Every Dollar Countz LLC
All rights reserved. This book or any portion thereof
may not be reproduced or used in any manner whatsoever
without the express written permission of the publisher
except for the use of brief quotations in a book review.

TABLE OF CONTENTS

27 MAE JEMISON

67 DONALD GLOVER

17 KETANJI B JACKSON

3 Booker T Washington	67 Donald Glover	131 Stephen A Smith
11 Ethel Hedgemon Lyle	75 Robin Roberts	139 Ida B Wells
19 William Hinton	83 W.E.B. Du Bois	147 Mary McLeod Bethune
27 Mae Jemison	91 Katherine Johnson	155 Alexa Irene Canady
35 James McCune	99 Carter G Woodson	163 Fern Hunt
43 Mary Eliza Mahon	107 Shonda Rhimes	171 Ketanji B Jackson
51 Benjamin Banneker	115 Michael Wilbon	179 Daryl E Evans
59 Fanny M Jackson	123 Rebecca L Crumpler	187 Bessie Coleman
		195 John W. Cromwell Jr

These Workbooks are geared to intrigue, inspire and motivate you to want to learn more about these Black Historical Figures(BHFs) and others. Also to do more research on your own. We know this isn't all the history of these individuals. We want you to do some of the research also. We try to be as accurate as possible during our research. If there are some stories or questions that aren't as stated, please contact us at info@wegonnalearntoday.com.

Booker T. Washington

Booker T. Washington

April 5, 1856 – November 14, 1915
EDUCATOR

LEFT BLANK ON PURPOSE

Booker T. Washington

Booker T. Washington

Booker T. Washington

Booker T. Washington

Booker T. Washington

Booker T. Washington

Directions: read the bio below and answer the following questions.

Hi, my name is Booker Washington. I was born on April 5, 1856, in Hale's Ford, VA. I went to Hampton Normal and Agricultural Institute (which was a historically Black college and is now Hampton University) and attended college at Wayland Seminary (which is now Virginia Union University). In 1881, this school became Tuskegee Normal and Industrial Institute (which is now Tuskegee University). I was the first school president at 25. A couple of decades later, in 1900, I started the National Negro Business League (NNBL) to inspire the "commercial, agricultural, educational and industrial advancement" of African Americans. In 1895, my Atlanta Exposition address was viewed as a "revolutionary moment" by both African Americans and white people across the country. After that address, I was often asked for political advice by presidents Theodore Roosevelt and William Howard Taft. In 1940, I became the first African American to be depicted on a United States postage stamp.

1. **What did I found in 1900?**
   A. NAACP
   B. NNBL
   C. CORE
2. **I became President of Tuskegee University in?**
   A. 1881
   B. 1890
   C. 1900
3. **I was the first African American in the U.S. to what?**
   A. Be Freed
   B. Be a millionaire
   C. Be on a U.S. postage stamp

Directions: Answer the questions, to solve the crossword puzzle. You can use the internet if you get stuck on any question.

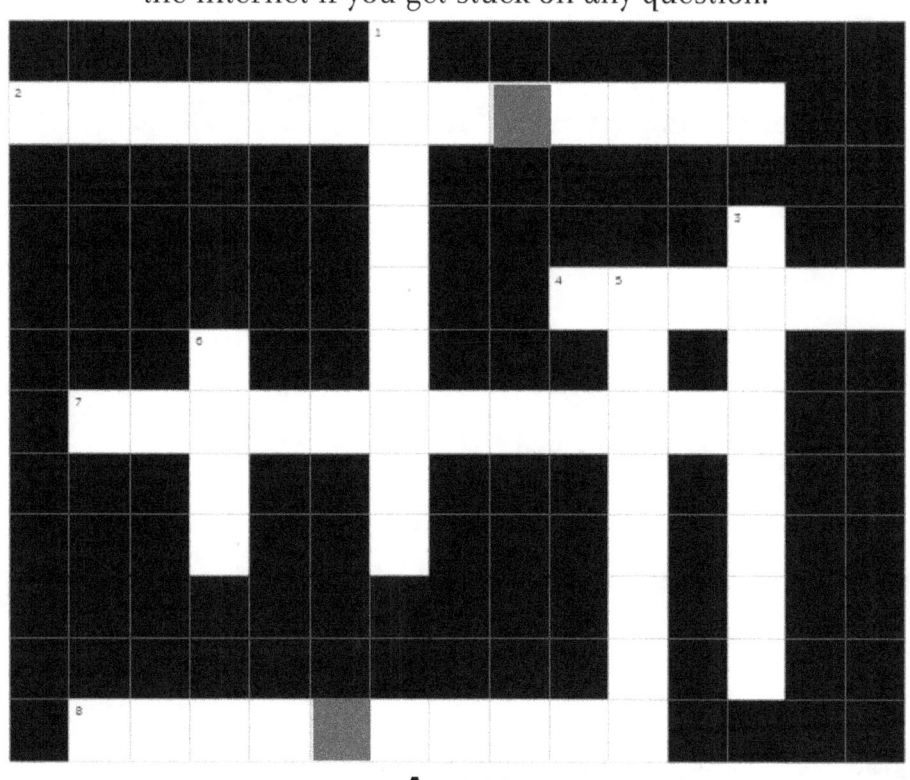

Across

2) Booker lectured at _____ in New York to raise money for the Tuskegee Institute.

4) Booker's students pretty much built their own _____ and grew their own crops.

7) Booker was born a slave but was freed when he was nine thanks to the _____ Proclamation.

8) Booker was a great orator sharing the stage with _____ and Robert Curtis Ogden sometimes.

Down

1) Booker set out to help Blacks to achieve education, _____ power and understanding of the U.S. legal system.

3) Booker was one of the _____ of the National Negro Business League.

5) Booker was part of a program that helped create 5,000 schools for Black _____ in rural communities.

6) Booker was an advisor to multiple U.S. Presidents like President _____.

Directions: read and answer the questions. These are your opinions so the answers will vary.

Would you rather go camping or stay in a hotel?

What's your favorite season & why?

What career are you most interested in? Why?

Directions: Unscramble the words below about Booker. See if you can get the bonus word.

BONUS WORD

| 1 | 2 | 3 | 4 | 5 | 6 | 7 | 8 | | 9 | 10 | 11 | 12 | 13 |

| 14 | 15 | 16 | 17 | 18 | 19 | 20 | 21 |

| 22 | 23 | 24 | 25 | 26 | 27 |

Unscramble Words

1) roarot
2) sivrade
3) rdatoecu
4) eskiietnesttugeut
5) cnuplaberi
6) tniiostatnetmpuh
7) ersriotdlneevepsto
8) cmrnmaptloaetiaso
9) agrenirlttisuttciulau
10) yevlars

9

Directions: This is the WGLT Challenge. Solve the cryptogram. As the puzzle solver, you need to find which number belongs to which character. And this can be pretty challenging! You will need to match the number with the letter. There are some letters given to you below. This will help you solve the other words and unlock more characters. **Good Luck.**

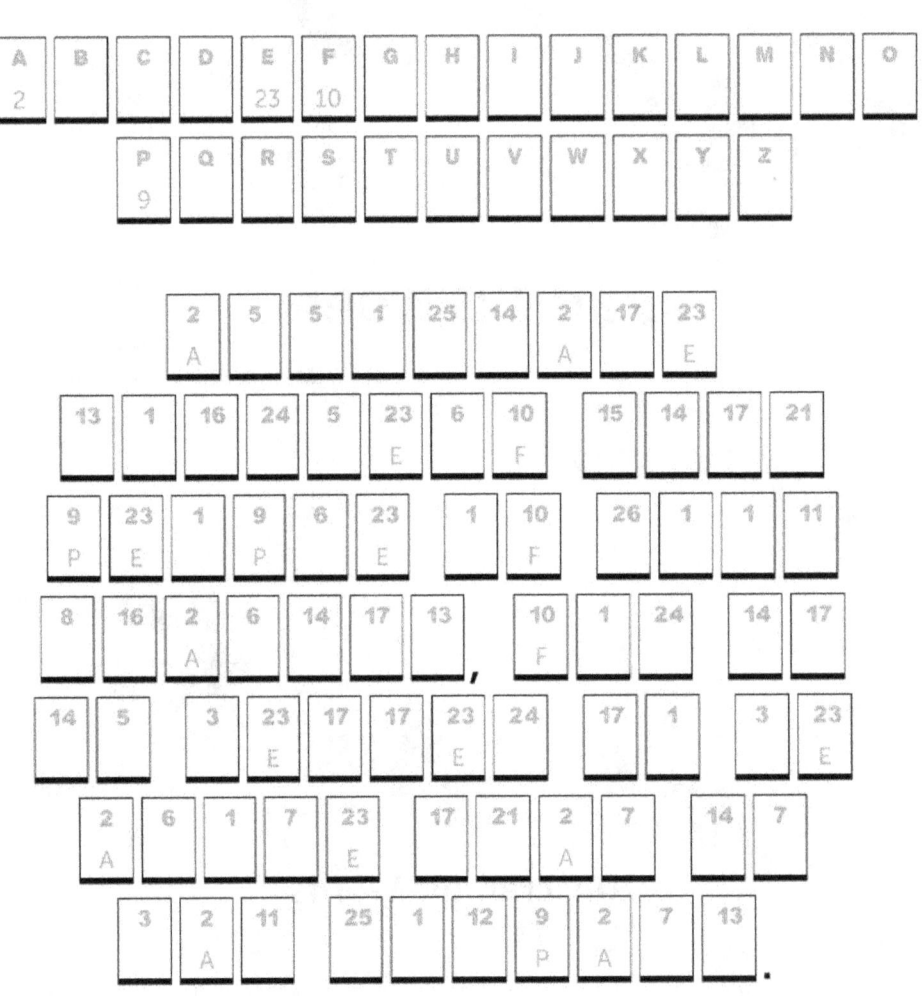

Ethel Hedgemon Lyle

Ethel Hedgemon Lyle

February 10, 1887 - November 28, 1950
EDUCATOR

LEFT BLANK ON PURPOSE

Ethel Hedgemon Lyle

Ethel Hedgemon Lyle

Ethel Hedgemon Lyle

Ethel Hedgemon Lyle

Ethel Hedgemon Lyle

Ethel Hedgemon Lyle

Directions: read the bio below and answer the following questions.

Hi, my name is Ethel Hedgemon. I was born on February 10, 1887, in St. Louis, MO. I graduated from Sumner High School with honors. I received a scholarship to Howard University, which is where I graduated from in 1907 with a Bachelor of Arts in Liberal Arts. I went to Howard at a time when only one in three hundred African Americans and 5% of whites of eligible age attended any college. In 1907, I was 20 when I came up with the idea for the Alpha Kappa Alpha Sorority Incorporated, which was the U.S.'s first Greek-letter organization that was established by Black college women. In 1908, eight classmates and I founded Alpha Kappa Alpha (AKA). I found my first teaching job in Oklahoma. I was the first African American female college graduate to teach in a normal school in Oklahoma and the first to earn a Teacher's Life Certificate from the Oklahoma State Department of Education.

1. What college did I graduate from?
   A. Howard University
   B. Alabama State University
   C. Jackson State University
2. What sorority did I found in 1908?
   A. Delta Sigma Theta
   B. Alpha Kappa Alpha
   C. Zeta Phi Beta
3. What was my Bachelors Degree in?
   A. Science
   B. Mathematics
   C. Liberal Arts

14

Directions: Find the words associated with Ethel's life and career.

D	X	A	L	P	H	A	K	A	P	P	A	A	L	P	H	A	B
U	Z	V	M	G	E	K	I	I	N	T	O	M	T	O	T	R	C
G	R	Q	N	N	J	A	L	T	R	Z	J	Q	G	K	P	Y	L
N	F	Z	J	E	C	Z	R	Q	D	U	F	W	A	B	M	T	S
R	U	V	Y	D	R	C	U	L	B	L	A	I	F	Q	A	I	P
Y	G	V	U	N	E	E	R	G	S	R	H	P	N	C	G	S	B
J	L	D	R	Y	F	I	F	E	S	P	A	V	M	Y	X	R	O
F	O	N	V	L	J	V	B	K	L	G	A	F	S	W	Q	E	X
Y	O	U	G	Z	K	L	W	E	D	A	N	T	A	N	N	V	O
M	H	K	F	R	N	J	D	P	P	O	R	U	A	A	A	I	F
K	C	O	V	C	Q	A	I	C	S	A	T	J	G	E	X	N	G
E	S	W	V	J	L	N	G	I	L	R	M	N	Y	V	I	U	V
H	L	V	L	I	K	I	B	A	S	H	T	H	F	C	Y	D	W
G	A	O	H	Q	Q	L	R	K	Y	A	T	V	S	Y	R	R	R
O	M	P	M	T	G	E	K	S	E	U	E	G	E	X	V	A	C
L	R	A	T	O	B	W	P	C	W	P	J	A	Q	O	T	W	N
D	O	D	W	I	Q	K	H	P	E	U	F	A	U	L	A	O	E
H	N	P	L	S	X	G	L	R	M	L	G	T	V	L	K	H	A

Find These Words

PHILADELPHIA	GREEN	BISON
EUFAULA	PEARLS	ALPHAKAPPAALPHA
PINK	LIBERALARTS	HOWARDUNIVERSITY
NORMALSCHOOL		

Directions: Read and answer the questions. These are your opinions so the answers will vary.

Would you rather ride a bike or a scooter?

What's your favorite website to visit?

Share a special memory you shared with family.

16

Directions: Read and answer the questions below. There are clues in the puzzle to help you. Try and solve the cryptic message.

Clue for cryptic message: Ethel went here at one time.

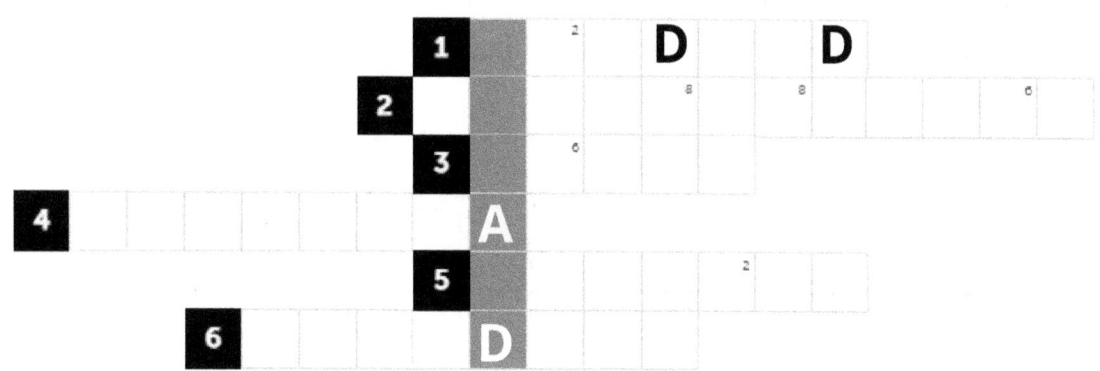

Questions

1) Ethel went to Howard at a time when only one in three _____ African Americans and 5% of whites of eligible age attended any college.

2) In 1937, Ethel helped organize a plan for the Sesquicentennial Anniversary of the Adoption of the U.S. _____.

3) ___ helped found civic institutions such as the West Philadelphia League of Women Voters

4) Ethel designed the _____ for the sorority.

5) It took Ethel about a year to ____ classmates interested in forming the sorority.

6) Ethel is a _____ member of Alpha Kappa Alpha.

Directions: This is the WGLT Challenge. Solve the cryptogram. As the puzzle solver, you need to find which number belongs to which character. And this can be pretty challenging! You will need to match the number with the letter. There are some letters given to you below. This will help you solve the other words and unlock more characters. **Good Luck.**

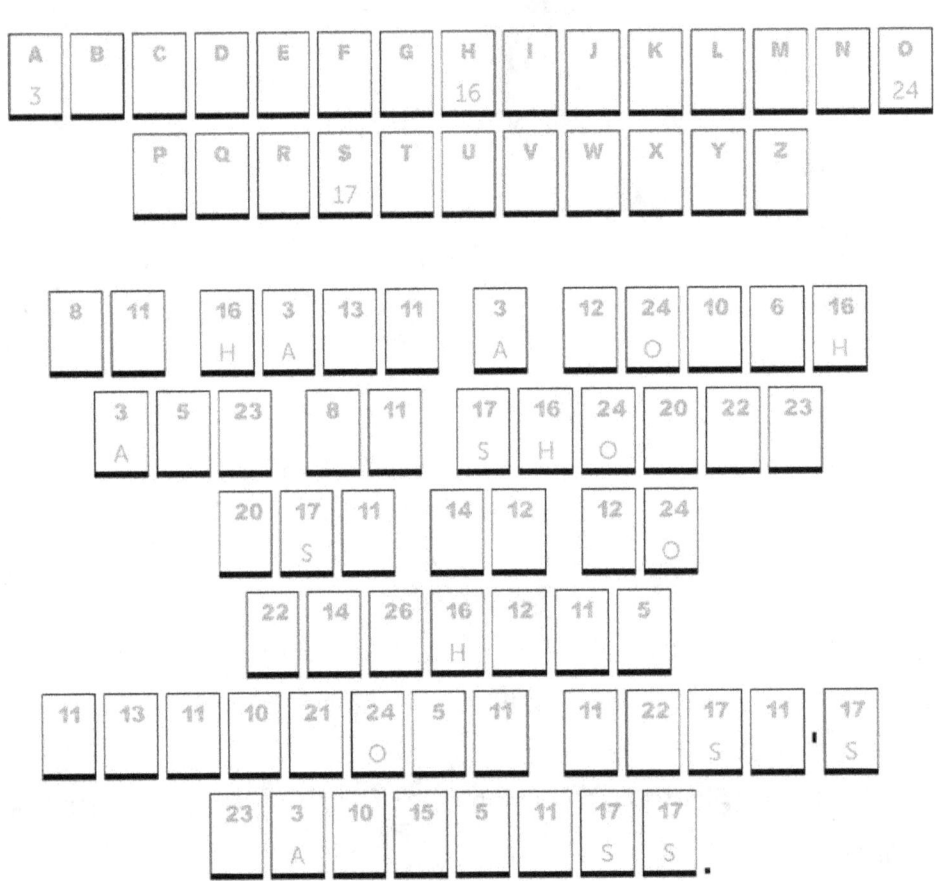

William Augustus Hinton

December 15, 1883 – August 8, 1959
BACTERIOLOGIST/PATHOLOGIST/EDUCATOR

LEFT BLANK ON PURPOSE

William Augustus Hinton

William Augustus Hinton

William Augustus Hinton

William Augustus Hinton

William Augustus Hinton

William Augustus Hinton

Directions: read the bio below and answer the following questions.

Hi, my name is William Hinton. I was born on December 15, 1883, in Chicago, IL. I grew up in Kansas, which is where I graduated from high school. I went to Harvard University; I got my bachelor's degree in 1905. I graduated from Harvard Medical School in 1912. I was denied a medical internship due to my race, so I worked as a "voluntary assistant" in the Pathology Laboratory at Massachusetts General Hospital. It was in this position that I became an expert on syphilis. I created what is called the Hinton test for syphilis, which proved to be more accurate than other tests that were accepted at that time and my test was endorsed by the U.S. Public Health Service in 1934. In 1918, I became an instructor in preventive medicine and hygiene at Harvard Medical School. In 1921, I became the first Black scientist to become a member of the American Society for Microbiology. Harvard appointed me as a clinical professor of bacteriology and immunology, which made me the first African American to be appointed as a professor at the university.

1. What was the name of the test I created for syphilis?
    A. Syphilis test
    B. Hinton test
    C. Chemiluminescence immunoassays test
2. What college did I graduate from?
    A. Yale
    B. Harvard
    C. Princeton
3. I was the first Black scientist to become a member of?
    A. National Honor Society
    B. American Society of Addiction Medicine
    C. American Society for Microbiology

Directions: Answer the questions, to solve the crossword puzzle. You can use the internet if you get stuck on any question.

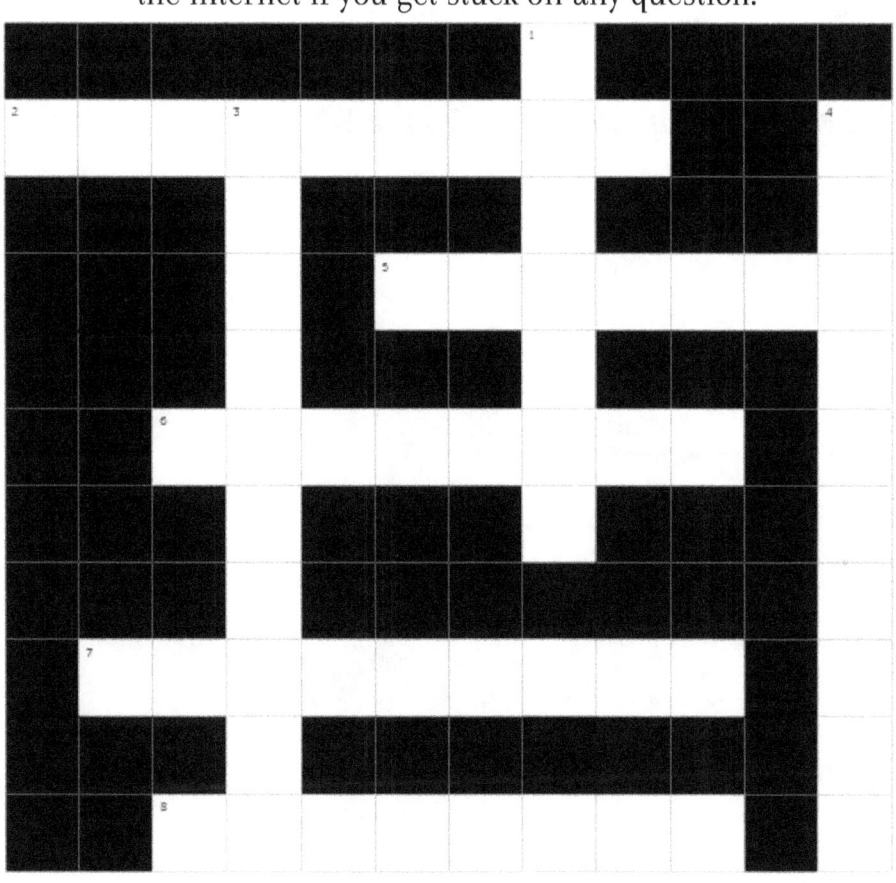

Across

2) William _____ the first medical textbook by a Black American: Syphilis and Its Treatment in 1936.
5) William was elected a life member of the American Social _____ Association.
6) William has a Harvard _____ scholarship fund named after President Dwight D. Eisenhower.
7) William was the first Black _____ in the history of Harvard University.
8) William developed a test for _____ which was very accuracy and used by the United States Public Health Service.

Down

1) William became the first Black person to write a _____ textbook in the U.S.
3) William was the Chief of the Wasserman _____ of the Massachusetts Department of Public Health.
4) William was an instructor in _____ medicine and hygiene at Harvard Medical School.

Directions: Read and answer the questions. These are your opinions so the answers will vary.

Would you rather stay up late or go to bed early?

What's your favorite movie?

Where do you hope to live someday?

Directions: Unscramble the words below about William. See if you can get the bonus word.

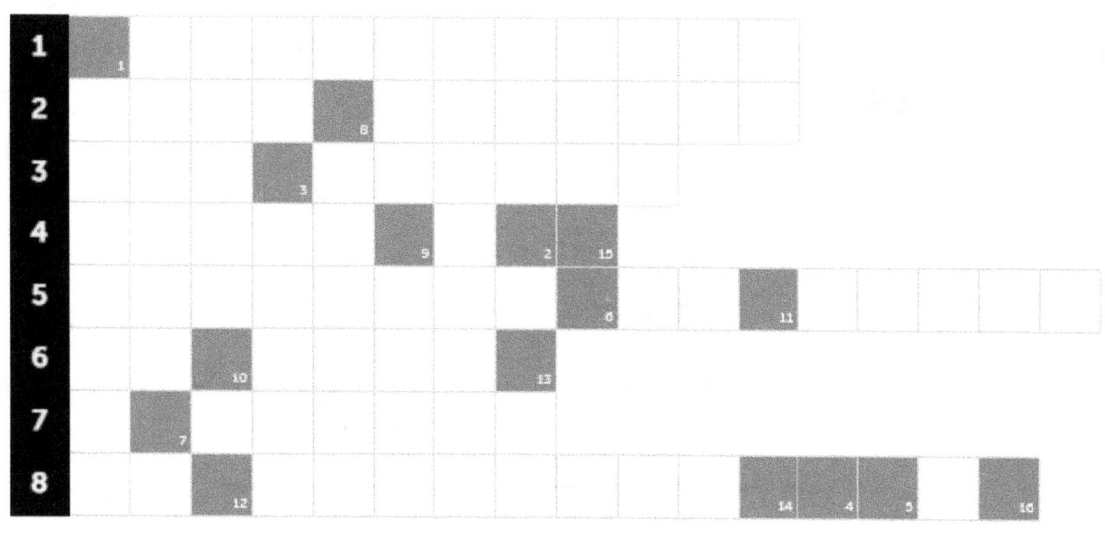

BONUS WORD

Unscramble Words

1) ilorbeygacto
2) huiptcbalhel
3) ygphoiylos
4) profsoers
5) haviursyednrirvta
6) sshpylii
7) oaucdetr
8) ahronaytlbtnioor

Directions: This is the WGLT Challenge. Solve the cryptogram. As the puzzle solver, you need to find which number belongs to which character. And this can be pretty challenging! You will need to match the number with the letter. There are some letters given to you below. This will help you solve the other words and unlock more characters. **Good Luck.**

Mae Carol Jemison

Mae Carol Jemison

October 17, 1956 - PRESENT
ENGINEER/NASA ASTRONAUT

27

LEFT BLANK ON PURPOSE

Mae Carol Jemison

Mae Carol Jemison

Mae Carol Jemison

Mae Carol Jemison

Mae Carol Jemison

Mae Carol Jemison

Directions: read the bio below and answer the following questions.

Hi, my name is Mae Jemison. I was born on October 17, 1956, in Decatur, AL. I graduated from Chicago's Morgan Park High School in 1973 and I entered Stanford University at the age of 16. I graduated from Stanford University with degrees in chemical engineering and African and African American studies. I earned my medical degree from Cornell University. I was a doctor for the Peace Corps in Liberia and Sierra Leone from 1983 until 1985 and worked as a general practitioner. In 1987, I became the first Black woman astronaut. I flew my only space mission from September 12 to 20, 1992, on STS-47. This was a cooperative mission between the United States and Japan, as well as the 50th shuttle mission. I logged 190 hours, 30 minutes and 23 seconds in space and orbited the earth 127 times. I became the first Black woman to travel into space.

1. What college did I get my medical degree from?
    A. Cornell University
    B. Stanford University
    C. Harvard University
2. How old was I when I started college?
    A. 18
    B. 16
    C. 19
3. I was the first African American woman to what?
    A. Fly a plane
    B. Travel into space
    C. Teach at Cornell University

Directions: Find the words associated with Mae's life and career.

S	V	H	E	O	C	P	G	D	Q	W	O	S	H	N	K	P	C
H	T	Z	B	O	P	R	L	U	V	U	M	A	Z	H	Y	T	O
G	N	A	D	W	F	F	A	O	K	K	L	U	E	B	A	V	R
Y	J	E	N	D	G	R	R	D	V	L	Q	S	J	U	I	M	N
G	H	L	A	F	E	H	F	I	O	I	T	T	J	J	P	V	E
O	G	T	T	B	O	D	P	F	I	A	R	I	A	S	L	O	L
L	7	U	T	V	X	R	F	H	R	P	M	T	Y	E	D	P	L
O	4	A	X	S	D	A	D	T	F	H	R	A	B	A	K	G	U
I	-	N	D	M	M	Y	R	U	N	Y	D	Z	J	C	C	D	N
S	S	O	P	E	V	E	V	T	N	S	R	S	Z	S	A	U	I
Y	T	R	X	D	K	N	S	E	T	I	N	Z	G	N	N	K	V
H	S	T	O	D	Z	J	C	P	X	C	V	H	C	M	D	V	E
P	Y	S	F	Q	Q	A	L	P	N	I	V	E	S	T	E	X	R
N	V	A	T	H	P	V	B	L	T	A	R	K	R	I	I	U	S
A	C	B	F	S	B	P	M	N	Q	N	S	Q	Q	S	W	M	I
M	S	T	G	X	W	V	X	I	D	B	G	U	O	V	I	G	T
U	M	N	V	A	P	S	C	S	R	A	I	E	C	O	L	T	Y
H	T	T	V	Y	A	E	Q	X	J	Y	E	V	M	B	H	T	Y

Find These Words

ASTRONAUT   STS-47   PHYSICIAN
HALLOFFAME   STARTREK   STANFORDUNIVERSITY
DANCER   HUMANPHYSIOLOGY   SPACE
CORNELLUNIVERSITY

Directions: Read and answer the questions. These are your opinions so the answers will vary.

Would you rather play video games or play outside?

What's your favorite vegetable or fruit?

Describe the most beautiful place you've ever been.

Directions: Read and answer the questions below. There are clues in the puzzle to help you. Try and solve the cryptic message.

Clue for cryptic message: Mae road in one of these.

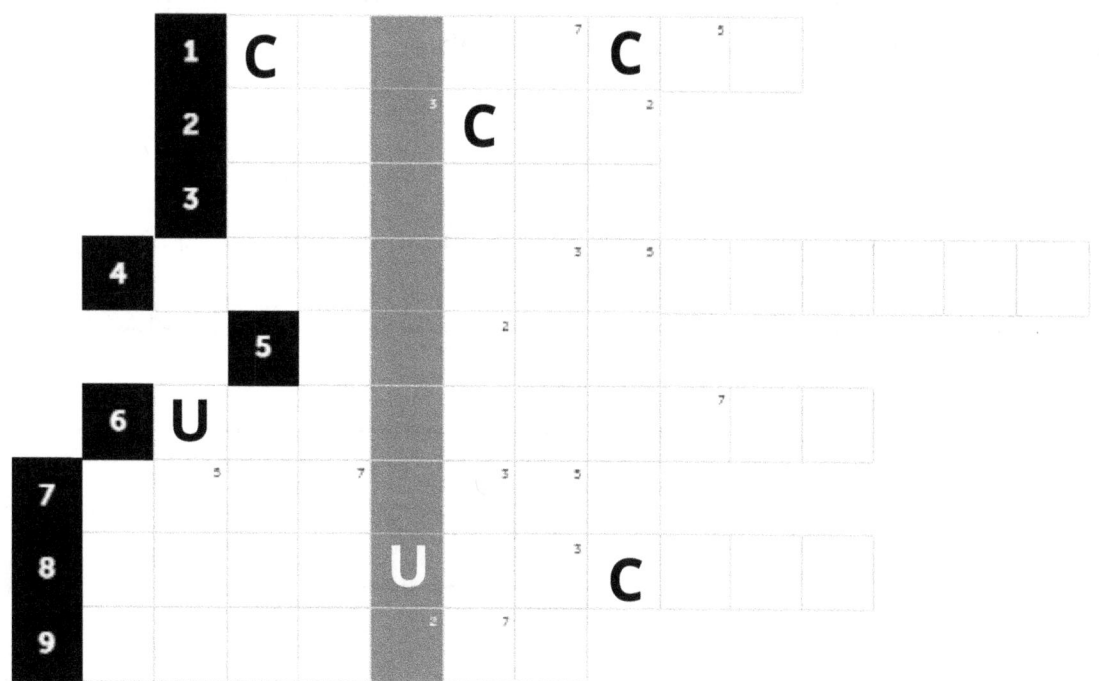

Questions

1) Mae studied _____ engineering at Stanford University.
2) Mae is a trained _____.
3) Mae learned several styles of dance, including African and Japanese, as well as ballet, jazz and _____ dance.
4) Mae is inducted into the _____ Space Hall of Fame.
5) Mae founded The _____ We Share (TEWS).
6) Mae earned her medical degree from Cornell _____.
7) Mae is inducted into the _____ Women's Hall of Fame.
8) Mae began communications on her shift with the salute "Hailing _____ open", a quote from Star Trek.
9) Mae was a doctor for the Peace Corps in _____ and Sierra Leone.

Directions: This is the WGLT Challenge. Solve the cryptogram. As the puzzle solver, you need to find which number belongs to which character. And this can be pretty challenging! You will need to match the number with the letter. There are some letters given to you below. This will help you solve the other words and unlock more characters. **Good Luck.**

James McCune Smith

James McCune Smith

April 18, 1813 – November 17, 1865
PHYSICIAN

LEFT BLANK ON PURPOSE

James McCune Smith

James McCune Smith

James McCune Smith

James McCune Smith

James McCune Smith

James McCune Smith

Directions: read the bio below and answer the following questions.

Hi, my name is James McCune Smith. I was born on April 18, 1813, in Manhattan, NY. I attended the African Free School (AFS). I also studied at the University of Glasgow in Scotland. I obtained a bachelor's degree in 1835, a master's degree in 1836 and a medical degree in 1837. I completed an internship in Paris. I was the first African American to hold a medical degree from the University of Glasgow in Scotland. I returned to the U.S. and established my practice in general surgery and medicine. I became the first African American to run a pharmacy in the United States. In 1846, I was appointed as the only physician at the Colored Orphan Asylum. I was a member of the American Anti-Slavery Society with Frederick Douglass. I helped Douglass start the National Council of Colored People in 1853, which was the first permanent national organization for Black people. In 1863, I was appointed as a professor of anthropology at Wilberforce College, which was the first African-American-owned and operated college in the United States.

1. **What is my highest level of education?**
    A. Ph. D
    B. Masters Degree
    C. Bachelors Degree
2. **I was the first African American in U.S. to what?**
    A. To travel to a different country
    B. To go to college overseas
    C. To run a pharmacy
3. **Where did I go to college at?**
    A. United States
    B. Scotland
    C. England

Directions: Answer the questions, to solve the crossword puzzle. You can use the internet if you get stuck on any question.

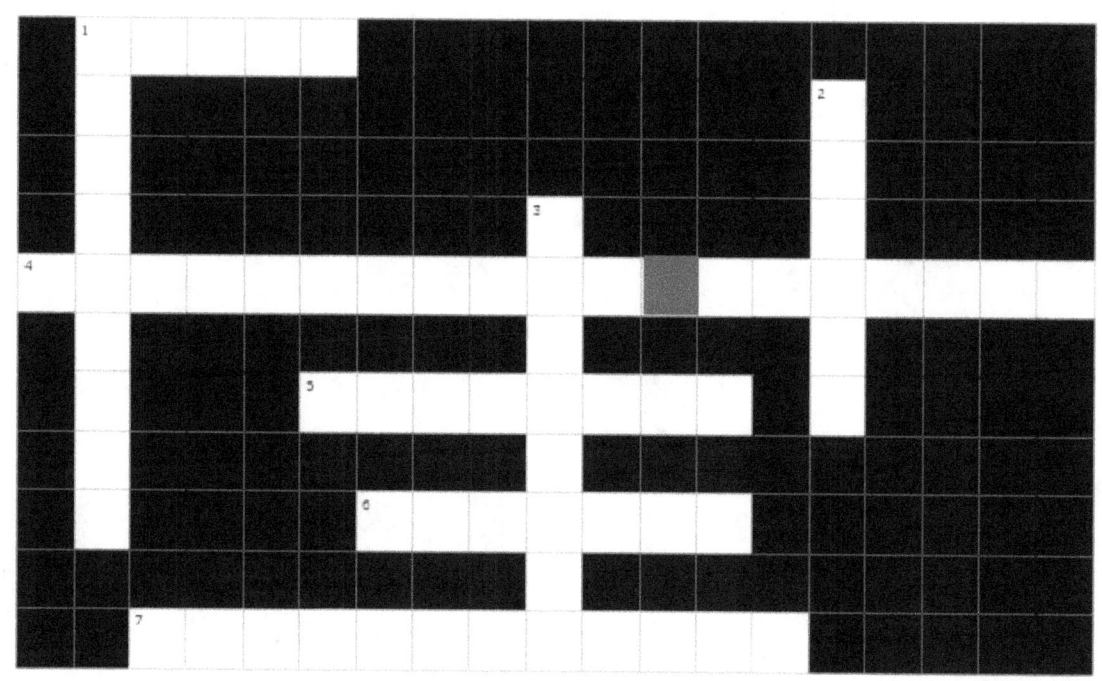

Across

1) James completed an internship in _____.
4) James was appointed as professor of anthropology at _____, the first African American-owned and operated college in the United States.
5) James aided _____ slaves to escape capture and helped connect them to people of the Underground Railroad and other escape routes.
6) James was the first African American to hold a ____ degree.
7) James was elected as a member by the American _____ Society.

Down

1) James was the first university-trained African-American _____ in the United States.
2) James worked as a physician for nearly 20 years at the Colored Orphan _____ in Manhattan.
3) James joined the Glasgow Emancipation Society and met people in the _____ and English abolitionist movement.

Directions: Read and answer the questions. These are your opinions so the answers will vary.

Would you rather get up early or sleep late?

What's your favorite activity to do at recess?

Share a special memory you had with a friend.

Directions: Unscramble the words below about James. See if you can get the bonus word.

BONUS WORD

Unscramble Words

1) anosiiiottlb
2) naipiscyh
3) rpoayathce
4) mlreuolsorpoahadncy
5) iwuanvrgytsloseig
6) rpsia
7) nloasctd
8) eicdlgedaerme

Directions: This is the WGLT Challenge. Solve the cryptogram. As the puzzle solver, you need to find which number belongs to which character. And this can be pretty challenging! You will need to match the number with the letter. There are some letters given to you below. This will help you solve the other words and unlock more characters. **Good Luck.**

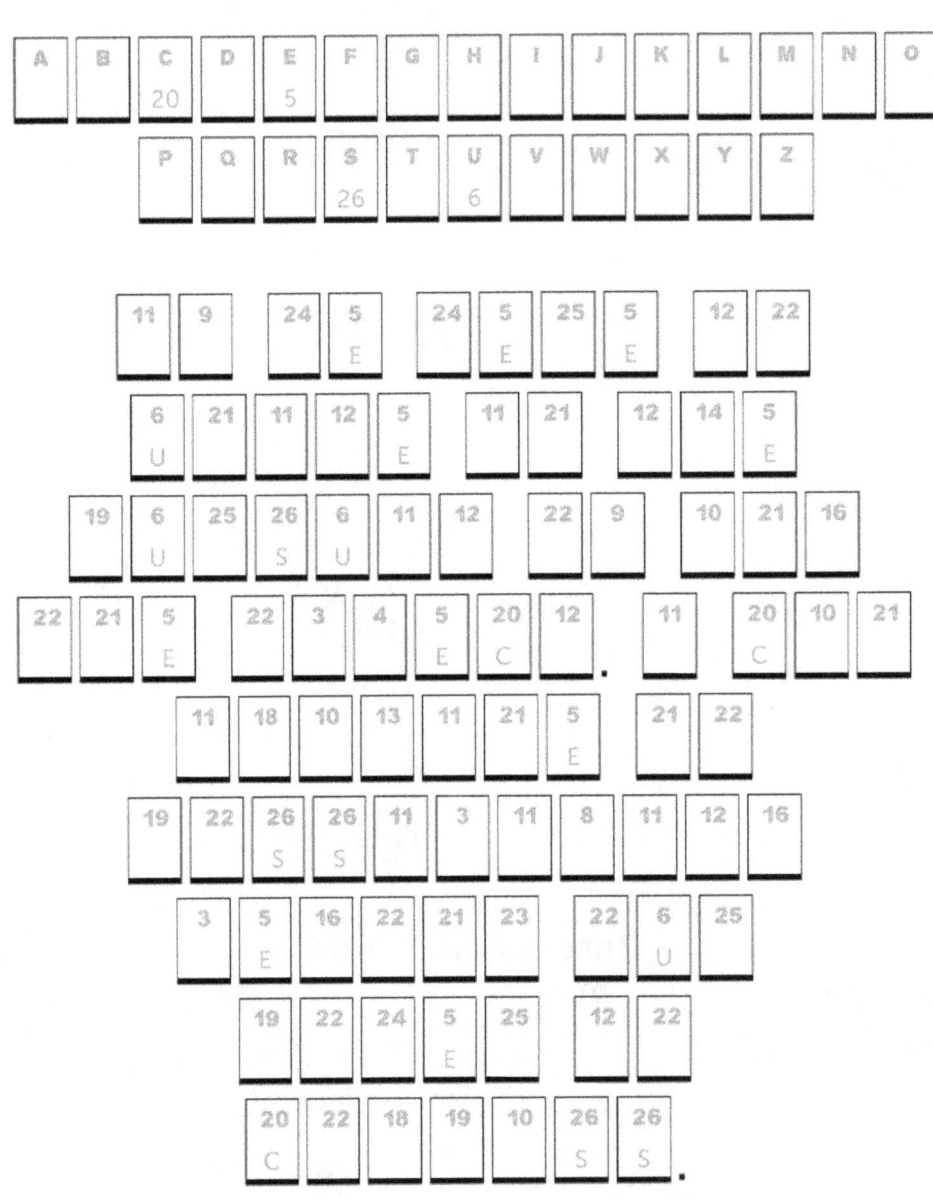

42

Mary Mahoney

Mary Mahoney

May 7, 1845 – January 4, 1926
NURSE

LEFT BLANK ON PURPOSE

Mary Mahoney

Mary Mahoney

Mary Mahoney

Mary Mahoney

Mary Mahoney

Mary Mahoney

Directions: read the bio below and answer the following questions.

Hi, my name is Mary Eliza Mahoney. I was born on May 7, 1845, in Dorchester, MA. I attended the Phillips School. Early on, I wanted to become a nurse because of the values that I learned about at school. I was admitted into a sixteen-month program at the New England Hospital for Women and Children (which is now the Dimock Community Health Center) in 1878 at the age of 33, along with thirty-nine other students. I graduated in 1879 as a registered nurse with three other colleagues and became the first Black woman to do so in the United States. I was also the first African American in the United States to study and work as a professionally trained nurse. In 1896, I became one of the original members of the then-predominantly white Nurses Associated Alumnae of the United States and Canada (NAAUSC), which later became the American Nurses Association (ANA). In 1908, I became the co-founder of the National Association of Colored Graduate Nurses (NACGN). This association didn't discriminate against anyone. The NACGN merged with the ANA in 1951.

1. In 1879 I graduated and became a what?
    A. Doctor
    B. Nurse
    C. Nurses Aid
2. What year did I help found NACGN?
    A. 1896
    B. 1908
    C. 1900
3. How long was the program to become a nurse?
    A. 12 months
    B. 6 months
    C. 16 months

46

Directions: Find the words associated with Mary's life and career.

```
H N K E R S F X J F Z N T X J M I D
M A R Y M A H O N E Y A W A R D L I
G R S Y I D E N T M Y V U Q K C C M
V L H B K H R U J S M V G X R T J O
D B D Q B B G R K J G X G W A L Q C
B A P T I S T S V I W N L I P M Y K
H E D I V E A E R B K N N P S S E H
E J Z F J H M M X D O A E N G X H E
L V A W Y M A N O C H S O E N Q U A
P V Q H L I I L I H Z U T J I N V L
K X M K U H D V L P T K F O K G O T
B P D N B S I Q V O Z H L A N C C H
Y A O P Y L D S D B F U A B T A Y C
V K I V W L W N Y S E F A D V N H E
F H J A H B R H R K K A A O A Y D N
D U R Y V E L F B T R J F M W L I T
S G A I N Q T N W V D X M E E R U E
G K V F Q Z C K K F W Q P F K I B R
```

Find These Words

KINGSPARK   NURSE   HALLOFFAME
CIVILWAR   DIMOCKHEALTHCENTER   ADAHTHOMAS
NACGN   BAPTIST   MARYMAHONEYAWARD
BOSTON

Directions: Read and answer the questions. These are your opinions so the answers will vary.

Would you rather ride a bike or a scooter?

What's your favorite book & why?

What are you most excited about doing when you are a teen then college student and then an adult?

Directions: Read and answer the questions below. There are clues in the puzzle to help you. Try and solve the cryptic message.

Clue for cryptic message: Mary performed as one of these.

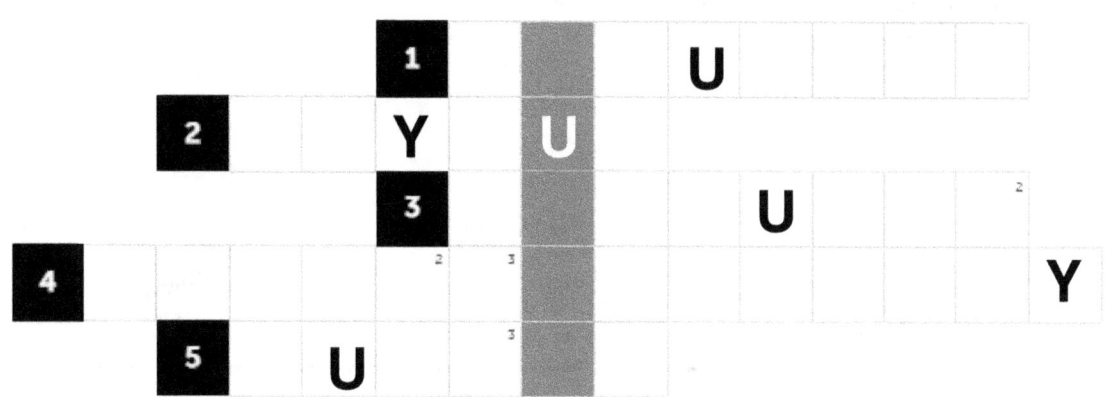

Questions

1) Mary was _____ into the National Women's Hall of Fame.
2) Mary served as director of the Howard Colored Orphan _____ for Black children in Kings Park, Long Island, NY.
3) In 1908, Mary co-founded the National Association of Colored _____ Nurses (NACGN).
4) Mary was the first African-American to study and work as a _____ trained nurse in the United States.
5) Mary was inducted into the American _____ Association Hall of Fame.

49

Directions: This is the WGLT Challenge. Solve the cryptogram. As the puzzle solver, you need to find which number belongs to which character. And this can be pretty challenging! You will need to match the number with the letter. There are some letters given to you below. This will help you solve the other words and unlock more characters. **Good Luck.**

50

Benjamin Banneker

Benjamin Banneker

November 9, 1731 – October 19, 1806
ASTRONOMER

LEFT BLANK ON PURPOSE

Benjamin Banneker

Benjamin Banneker

Benjamin Banneker

Benjamin Banneker

Benjamin Banneker

Benjamin Banneker

Directions: read the bio below and answer the following questions.

Hi, my name is Benjamin Banneker. I was born on November 9, 1731, in Baltimore County, Province of Maryland, British America. I was born a free African American, which was rare for this period. Peter Heinrichs, a Quaker, gave me access to his personal library. I also periodically attended Heinrichs' one-room school. However, I had to end my education when I was old enough to help on my family's farm. I primarily worked as a farmer throughout my life. I am known for doing several things. In 1791, I was selected to be part of a team that was led by Major Andrew Ellicott to survey the land that would eventually become Washington, D.C. My primary work there was to make astronomical observations. I published a series of almanacs annually from 1792 to 1797 and sold them in six cities in the four states. I also predicted the solar eclipse that occurred in 1789. In 1791, I wrote a letter to Thomas Jefferson, who was the U.S. Secretary of State at the time, to plead for justice for African Americans and received a response to my letter.

1. What State did I help survey?
    A. Virginia
    B. Delaware
    C. Washington D.C.
2. What did I successfully predict?
    A. The next President
    B. A Solar Eclipse
    C. The freeing of slaves
3. I primarily worked where?
    A. At the Capitol
    B. The farm
    C. With Major Ellicott

Directions: Answer the questions, to solve the crossword puzzle. You can use the internet if you get stuck on any question.

Across
4) Benjamin accurately forecasted lunar and _____.
7) Benjamin helped _____ for what is now known as Washington D.C.
8) Benjamin constructed an _____ system for the family farm

Down
1) Benjamin was born _____ which was not the norm at this time.
2) Benjamin was largely self-educated in _____ and mathematics.
3) Benjamin created a series of _____ for five years and was sold in four states.
5) Benjamin built a _____ clock that worked for over forty years.
6) Benjamin worked as a farmer on their 100-acre _____ farm.

Directions: Read and answer the questions. These are your opinions so the answers will vary.

Would you rather be a wizard or a superhero?

What's your favorite ice cream flavor?

Share a time when someone was extra kind to you.

Directions: Unscramble the words below about Benjamin. See if you can get the bonus word.

BONUS WORD

Unscramble Words

1) seryvla   **2)** aahmctniatime   **3)** yuaqaitcirllea
4) rtiaanslut   **5)** hefoorlk   **6)** seonrmraot
7) ruoryesv   **8)** amlcarnothuaa   **9)** ndalweorn

Directions: This is the WGLT Challenge. Solve the cryptogram. As the puzzle solver, you need to find which number belongs to which character. And this can be pretty challenging! You will need to match the number with the letter. There are some letters given to you below. This will help you solve the other words and unlock more characters. **Good Luck.**

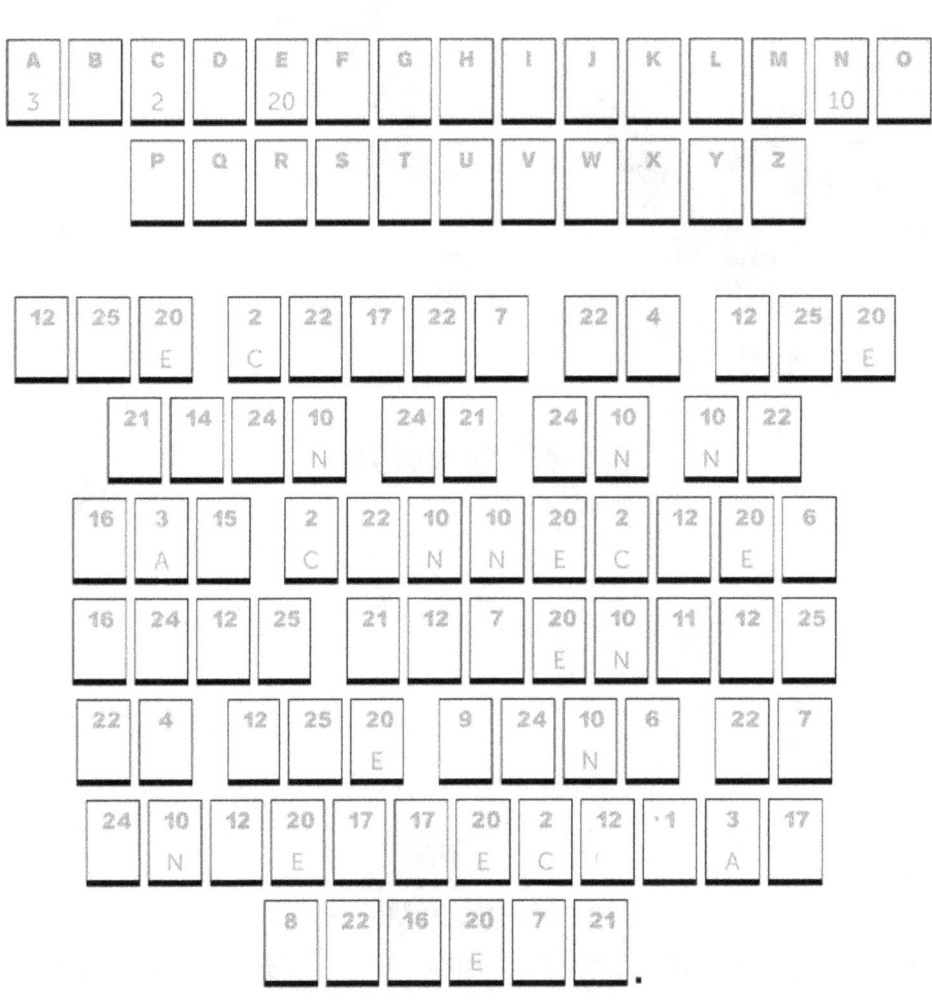

October 15, 1837 – January 21, 1913
EDUCATOR

LEFT BLANK ON PURPOSE

Fanny Jackson Coppin

Fanny Jackson Coppin

Fanny Jackson Coppin

Fanny Jackson Coppin

Fanny Jackson Coppin

Fanny Jackson Coppin

Directions: read the bio below and answer the following questions.

Hi, my name is Fanny Jackson Coppin. I was born on October 15, 1837, in Hale's Washington, D.C. I paid for tutoring with my own earnings and was able to enroll at Oberlin College in Ohio. Oberlin was the first college in the United States to accept both Black and female students. It was a custom at Oberlin to hire forty students from the junior and senior classes to teach the preparatory classes. I was the first Black teacher at the Oberlin Academy. While at Oberlin College, I taught an evening course on reading and writing for free African Americans and I graduated with a bachelor's degree in 1865. Later that year, I accepted a position at Philadelphia's Institute for Colored Youth. In 1869, I became the first African American woman to become a school principal. While I was a principal, I was promoted by the Board of Education to the rank of superintendent. I became the first African American superintendent of a school district in the United States.

1. **I wasn't the first African American woman to what?**
    A. Principal
    B. Superintendent
    C. Student
2. **What year did I graduate from college?**
    A. 1860
    B. 1863
    C. 1865
3. **I was the first African American to do what at Oberlin?**
    A. Graduate
    B. Teacher
    C. Valedictorian

Directions: Find the words associated with Fanny's life and career.

```
A N N I T A L M Z Z O T Z M R R S X
U M A X P S G F L C N R A V A Q R R
O Y U J H K F U P N R T B A T J P P
S P Z R U P W I H H H C N F P R C B
Q G G G R R M D L E H L S H I J G M
Q C D R L B P I M S O Q P N U R W D
A B H E S S K A L O U I C F E J H Z
Z D T E I F T R H T E I M H U V K F
A W Z K O I W C B O P J C Q D D R N
C Q A D C J S B M A W A B I I D O I
Z R Y S G R G V L W E I C B H L P M
P S I H E B L W S T V U N Y P B B T
H V A K S R V M I S S I O N A R Y V
H K A K J G D N M R I H V T T H V R
K U Z P L E C T U R E R P G M E I B
Q M D J H M M J E O Z C C L G E M R
L Q O B E R L I N C O L L E G E A V
F E I H A M E G H O D I S T N W U M
```

Find These Words

QUAKERSCHOOL   LATIN   PRINCIPAL
LECTURER   MISSIONARY   OBERLINCOLLEGE
MEGHODIST   GREEK   TEACHER
MATHEMATICS

Directions: Read and answer the questions. These are your opinions so the answers will vary.

Would you rather work in a group or work alone?

What's your favorite hobby or after school activity?

Where do you want to go to college?

Directions: Read and answer the questions below. There are clues in the puzzle to help you. Try and solve the cryptic message.

Clue for cryptic message: Fanny went to one of these.

Questions

1) Fanny was politically active her entire life and _____ spoke at political rallies.

2) Fanny performed a variety of missionary work in ____ Africa.

3) Fanny enrolled at Oberlin College, the first college in the United States to accept both black and _____ students

4) Fanny took a position at Philadelphia's Institute for Colored Youth and taught ____, Latin and Mathematics.

5) Fanny was one of the first vice _____ of the National Association of Colored Women.

6) Fanny was the first black teacher at the _____ Academy.

65

Directions: This is the WGLT Challenge. Solve the cryptogram. As the puzzle solver, you need to find which number belongs to which character. And this can be pretty challenging! You will need to match the number with the letter. There are some letters given to you below. This will help you solve the other words and unlock more characters. **Good Luck.**

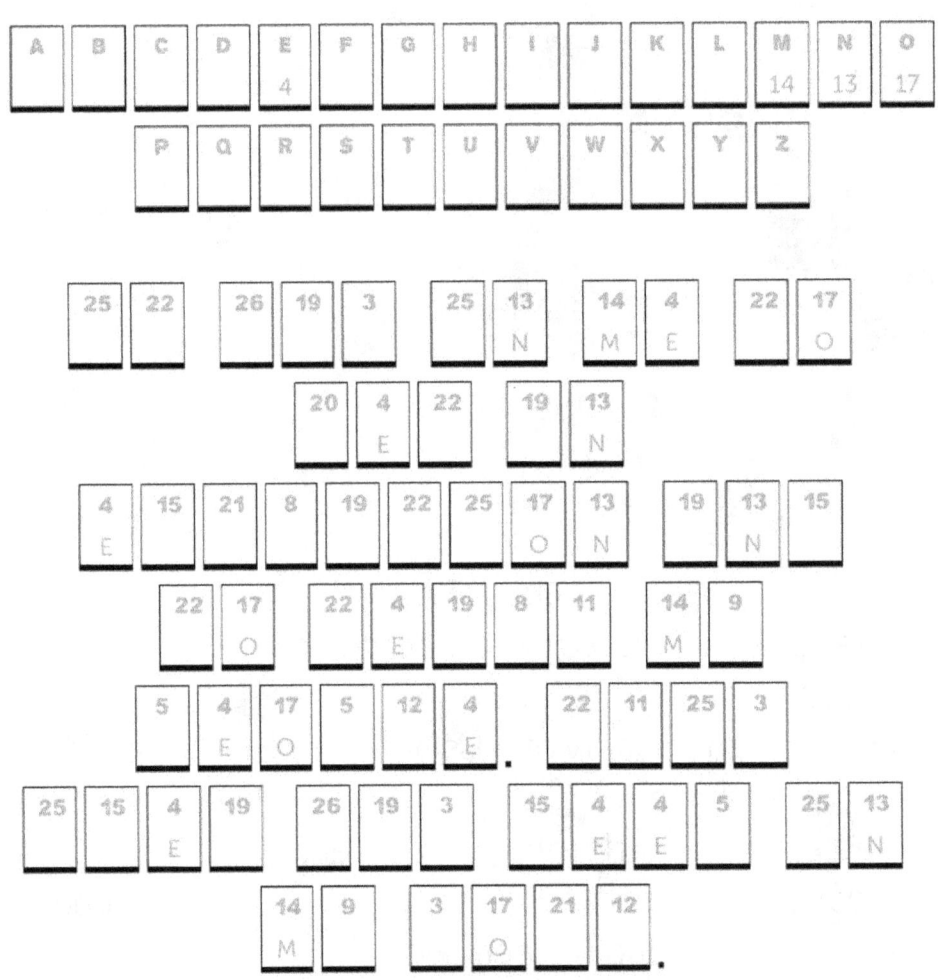

Donald Glover Jr

Donald Glover Jr

September 25, 1983 - PRESENT
DIRECTOR **67**

LEFT BLANK ON PURPOSE

Donald Glover Jr

Donald Glover Jr

Donald Glover Jr

Donald Glover Jr

Donald Glover Jr

Donald Glover Jr

Directions: read the bio below and answer the following questions.

Hi, my name is Donald Glover Jr. I was born on September 25, 1983, at Edwards Air Force Base in Edwards, CA. I attended Avondale High School and DeKalb School of the Arts. In 2006, I graduated from the New York University Tisch School of the Arts with a bachelor's degree in dramatic writing. From 2006 to 2009, I wrote for 30 Rock and I also had occasional cameo appearances. We won the Writers Guild of America Award for Best Comedy Series in 2008 for our work on the third season. I starred in the sitcom Community in 2009. Some of the movies, albums and TV series that I'm known for are Mystery Team (2009), Solo: A Star Wars Story (2018), Guava Island (2019), Community (2009–2014), Ultimate Spider-Man (2015), Atlanta (2016–present), Camp (2011), Awaken, My Love (2016) and 3.15.20 (2020).

1. What film did I act, write and produce?
   A. Guava Island
   B. Magic Mike XXL
   C. The To Do List
2. What college did I go to?
   A. UCLA
   B. University of Georgia
   C. New York University
3. What award did I win for writing on 30 Rock?
   A. Image Award
   B. Emmys
   C. Writers Guild of America Award

Directions: Answer the questions, to solve the crossword puzzle. You can use the internet if you get stuck on any question.

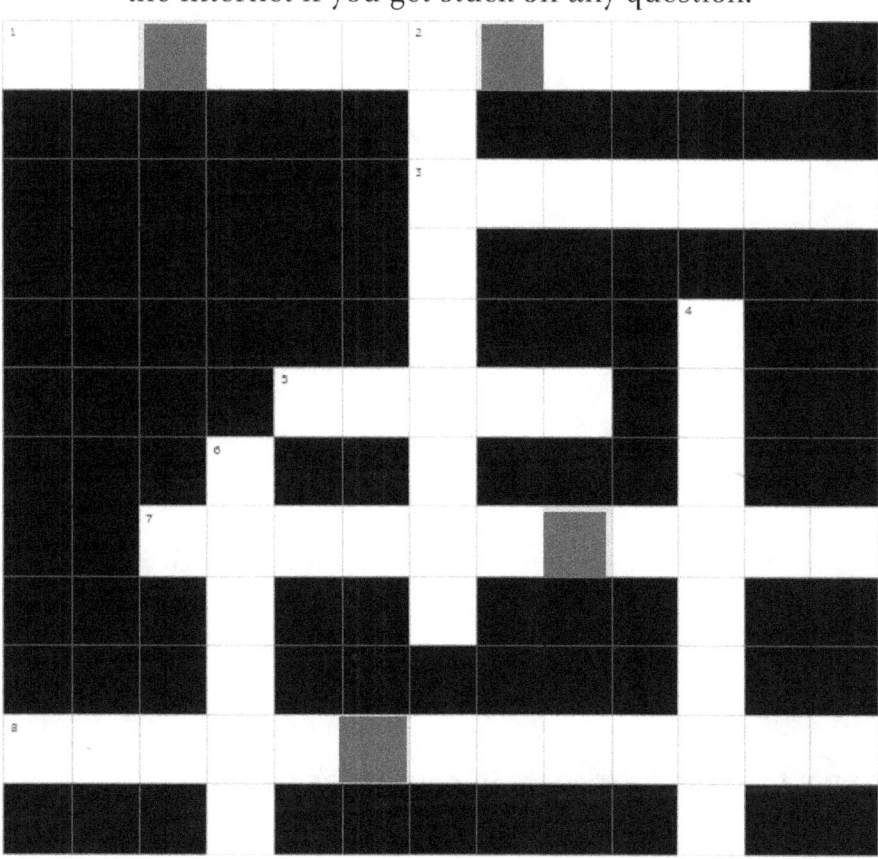

Across

1) Donald got his rap name from a _____ rap name generator,

3) _____ was the first time Donald wrote, acted, directed and was the executive producer.

5) Donald owned as a child _____ figure in the likeness of The Empire Strikes Back and Return of the Jedi's Billy Dee Williams.

7) Donald was an actor and writer on the show _____.

8) Donald had some insight on the _____ script and was acknowledged in Special Thanks credits of the movie.

Down

2) In 2011, Donald signed a record deal with _____ Records.

4) Donald was raised as a _____ witness.

6) Donald is real good friends with _____ the Rapper.

Directions: Read and answer the questions. These are your opinions so the answers will vary.

Would you rather play hide-and-seek or dodgeball?

What's your favorite meal of the day?

Share about a time you learned an important life lesson.

Directions: Unscramble the words below about Donald. See if you can get the bonus word.

BONUS WORD

Unscramble Words

1) ecpdurro   **2)** antaalt   **3)** eipsnerxoearhecp
4) prpear   **5)** alsdrannaciosli   **6)** davnalgsiua
7) irrwte   **8)** omeacnid   **9)** siabm
10) tiaismairehcs

Directions: This is the WGLT Challenge. Solve the cryptogram. As the puzzle solver, you need to find which number belongs to which character. And this can be pretty challenging! You will need to match the number with the letter. There are some letters given to you below. This will help you solve the other words and unlock more characters. **Good Luck.**

Robin Roberts

Robin Roberts

November 23, 1960 - PRESENT
TELEVISION BROADCASTER

LEFT BLANK ON PURPOSE

Robin Roberts

Robin Roberts

Robin Roberts

Robin Roberts

Robin Roberts

Robin Roberts

Directions: read the bio below and answer the following questions.

Hi, my name is Robin Roberts. I was born on November 23, 1960, in Tuskegee, AL. I attended Pass Christian High School and graduated as a member of the class of 1979 and I was the class salutatorian. I attended Southeastern Louisiana University and graduated cum laude in 1983 with a bachelor's degree in communication. In 1983, I started my career as a sports anchor and reporter for WDAM-TV in MS. In 1984, I moved to WLOX-TV in MS. In 1986, I was the sports anchor and reporter for WSMV-TV in TN. From 1988 to 1990, I was a sports anchor and reporter at WAGA-TV in GA. I was also a radio host for the radio station V-103. I joined ESPN as a sportscaster in February 1990, where I stayed until 2005. My catchphrase was, "Go on with your bad self!" In 1995, I was a featured reporter for Good Morning America (GMA). At the time, I was working for both ESPN and GMA. In 2005, I was promoted to co-anchor of GMA. In April 2022, I celebrated my 20th anniversary with GMA.

1. What was my first broadcasting job for?
   A. WLOX-TV
   B. WSMV-TV
   C. WDAM-TV
2. What year did I start working for GMA?
   A. 1995
   B. 2005
   C. 1990
3. What college did I graduate from?
   A. Southeastern Louisiana University
   B. Louisiana State University
   C. Tuskegee University

Directions: Find the words associated with Robin's life and career.

```
J B Y A D E H T Y B R E T H G I R B
R B V U H U D Q F Q R Q A P Y E F N
H A R L E M G L O B E T R O T T E R
E E U E I N O I L E H T E I M O O R
K B Q M T X L W K I J D R R G J Q F
V R O Q G N X T Z U Q D E I V Z C D
Y O Z F W Q E N R O R C G G O R Z A
A A R A Y L Q C P Q N H D I U C S N
J D V A S Z L S S A A W X A L J S P
V C S P L O G A C T F J N N Y V R O
A A V W A K S Q B E R C Q P M V A V
X S K T E L T N U T H O P J C U V U
N T N B W N J N W O E R P E H A V G
T E U N W W C K R S S K A S K N P P
C R O G C M U B Q R U C S B P W O X
T U W D I A E N A F E V T A T B E E
H P M A O W G Q N M X N D J B J U U
G O O D M O R N I N G A M E R I C A
```

Find These Words

BASKETBALL ANCHOR SPORTSCENTER
ROOMIETHELION GOODMORNINGAMERICA CANCER
BROADCASTER ABCNEWS BRIGHTERBYTHEDAY
HARLEMGLOBETROTTER

Directions: Read and answer the questions. These are your opinions so the answers will vary.

Would you rather have indoor or outdoor recess?

What's your favorite board or card game?

What do you think you might be doing in 10 years?

Directions: Read and answer the questions below. There are clues in the puzzle to help you. Try and solve the cryptic message.

Clue for cryptic message: Robin is apart of this now.

Questions

1) Robin was ESPN's first on-air African-American _____.

2) Robin earned a 2012 _____ Award for the coverage of her treatment for myelodysplastic syndrome.

3) Robin graduated cum _____ with a degree in communication.

4) Robin had her jersey number twenty-one retired from Southeastern _____ University.

5) Robin began her career as a _____ anchor and reporter for WDAM-TV.

6) Robin was a sportscaster on ESPN for ____ years.

7) Robin was inducted into the Women's Basketball Hall of ____.

8) Robin was a guest host on _____ for five episodes.

9) Robin anchors for ABC's Good _____ America.

10) Robin's dad was a pilot with the _____ Airmen in World War II.

81

Directions: This is the WGLT Challenge. Solve the cryptogram. As the puzzle solver, you need to find which number belongs to which character. And this can be pretty challenging! You will need to match the number with the letter. There are some letters given to you below. This will help you solve the other words and unlock more characters. **Good Luck.**

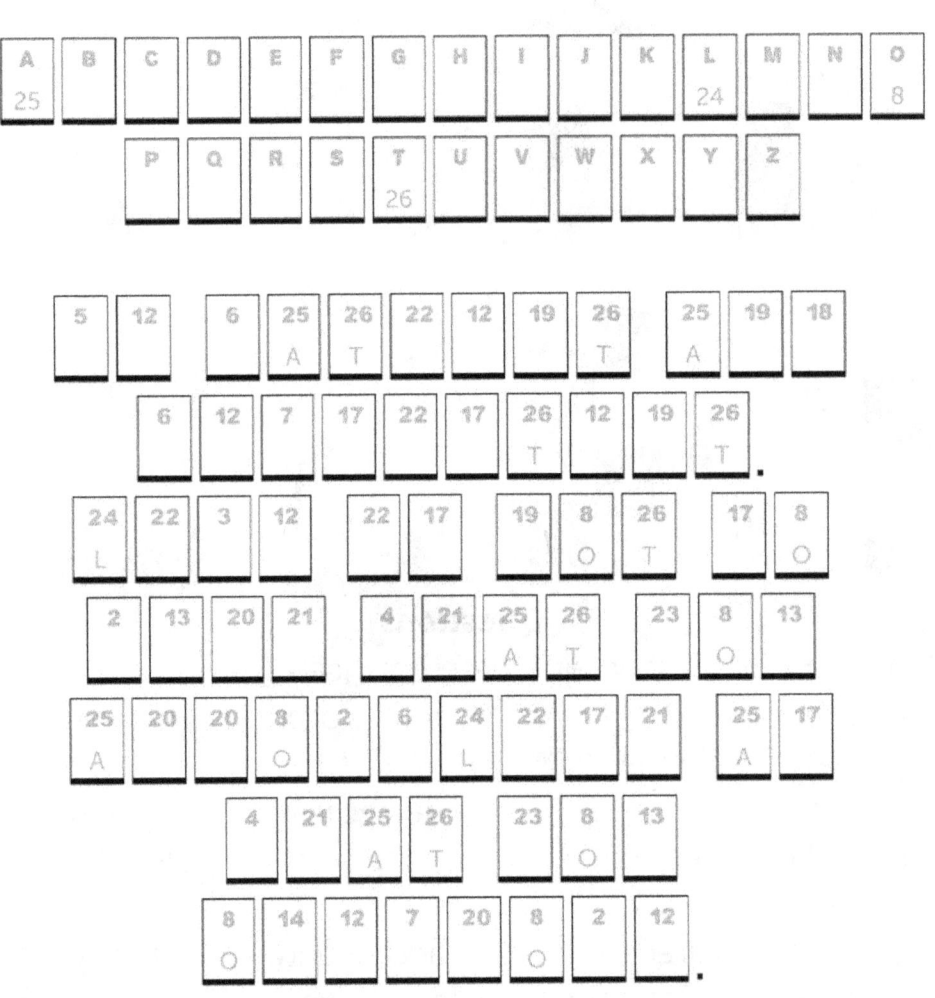

W. E. B. Du Bois

W. E. B. Du Bois

February 23, 1868 – August 27, 1963
SOCIOLOGIST/HISTORIAN

LEFT BLANK ON PURPOSE

W. E. B. Du Bois

W. E. B. Du Bois

W. E. B. Du Bois

W. E. B. Du Bois

W. E. B. Du Bois

W. E. B. Du Bois

Directions: read the bio below and answer the following questions.

Hi, my name is William Edward Burghardt Du Bois. I was born on February 23, 1868, in Great Barrington, MA. I graduated from Searles High School. I graduated with a bachelor's degree from Fisk University. In 1892, I attend the University of Berlin for graduate work. In 1895, I became the first African American to earn a Ph.D. from Harvard University. In 1897, I took a professorship in history and economics at the historically Black Atlanta University. I wrote the book The Philadelphia Negro (1899), which is a detailed and comprehensive sociological study of the African American people of Philadelphia and is based on my fieldwork from 1896–1897. This was the first scientific study of African Americans and a major contribution to early scientific sociology in the US. In 1909, a group of us founded the National Association for the Advancement of Colored People (NAACP) as an interracial endeavor to advance justice for African Americans.

1. I was the first African American to do what at Harvard?
   A. Get a Bachelors degree
   B. Get a Ph. D
   C. Get a Maters degree
2. What year did I co-found NACCP?
   A. 1900
   B. 1899
   C. 1909
3. What college did I get my Bachelors Degree from?
   A. University of Berlin
   B. Fisk University
   C. Harvard University

Directions: Answer the questions, to solve the crossword puzzle. You can use the internet if you get stuck on any question.

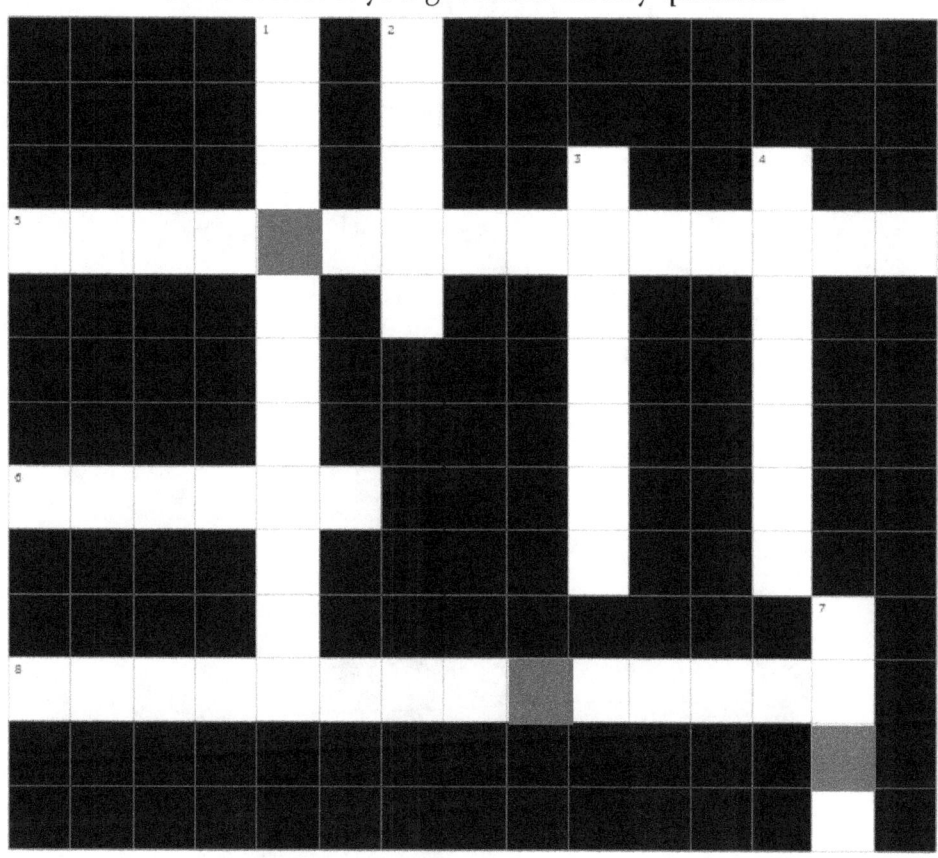

Across

5) W.E.B. Du Bois graduated from _____ with a bachelor's degree.
6) W.E.B. Du Bois was selected for a study-abroad program at the University of ____.
8) W.E.B. Du Bois coined the phrase "the _____," a term that described the likelihood of one in 10 Black men becoming leaders of their race.

Down

1) W.E.B. Du Bois helped organize multiple _____ Conferences to fight systemic racism and to end colonialism.
2) W.E.B. Du Bois was a citizen of _____.
3) W.E.B. Du Bois ran for U.S. ____ from New York on the American Labor Party ticket.
4) W.E.B. Du Bois founded the _____ Movement.
7) W.E.B. Du Bois was the first African American to get a ____.

Directions: Read and answer the questions. These are your opinions so the answers will vary.

Would you rather go to a zoo or an aquarium?

What's your favorite snack to eat?

Describe the most amazing thing you've ever seen in real life.

Directions: Unscramble the words below about W.E.B. Du Bois. See if you can get the bonus word.

BONUS WORD

Unscramble Words

1) isgcloioots
2) glrtihsviic
3) iesnnarcctoorreut
4) dacoetotr
5) ieccnmsoo
6) preorosfs
7) acpna
8) rnenrilibtfsyieuvo
9) soeildkcarbls
10) ufwaskondd

89

Directions: This is the WGLT Challenge. Solve the cryptogram. As the puzzle solver, you need to find which number belongs to which character. And this can be pretty challenging! You will need to match the number with the letter. There are some letters given to you below. This will help you solve the other words and unlock more characters. **Good Luck.**

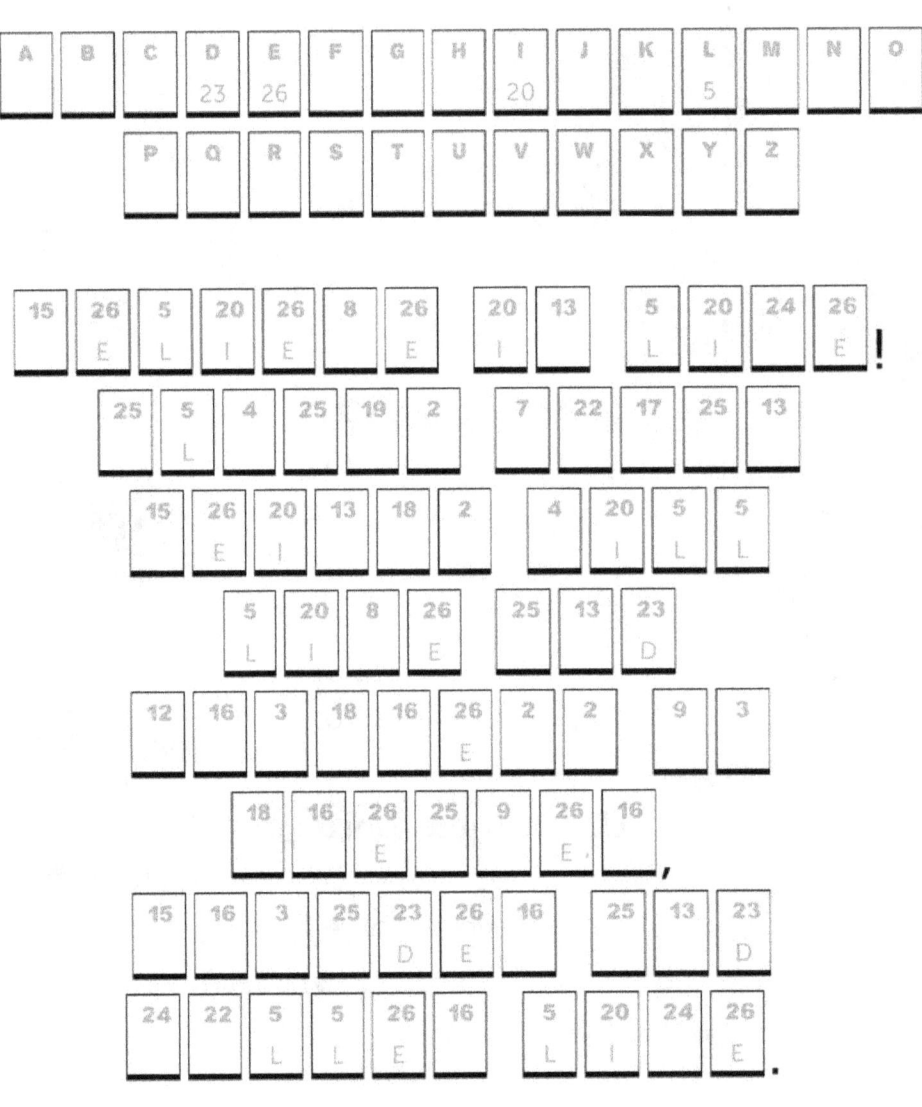

Katherine Johnson

91

August 26, 1918 – February 24, 2020
MATHEMATICIAN

LEFT BLANK ON PURPOSE

Katherine Johnson

Katherine Johnson

Katherine Johnson

Katherine Johnson

Katherine Johnson

Katherine Johnson

Directions: read the bio below and answer the following questions.

Hi, my name is Creola Katherine Coleman. I was born on August 26, 1918, in White Sulphur Springs, WV. I graduated from high school when I was 14. I graduated summa cum laude from West Virginia State College (WVSC) in 1937 with degrees in mathematics and French. I was also a member of the Alpha Kappa Alpha sorority. I was the first African American woman to attend graduate school at West Virginia University. In 1953, I worked for the National Advisory Committee for Aeronautics (NACA). In 1958, the agency was superseded by NASA. I was made an aerospace technologist in the Spacecraft Controls Branch. I calculated the trajectory for the May 5, 1961, space flight of Alan Shepard, who was the first U.S. citizen in space. I verified the computer's numbers at John Glenn's request. He had refused to fly unless I verified the calculations. I helped to calculate the trajectory for the 1969 Apollo 11 flight to the Moon and I got to watch the first steps being made on the Moon.

1. How old was I when I graduated college?
   A. 14
   B. 18
   C. 22
2. What year did I start working for NASA?
   A. 1953
   B. 1961
   C. 1958
3. What is the name of my sorority?
   A. Sigma Gamma Rho
   B. Zeta Phi Beta
   C. Alpha Kappa Alpha

Directions: Find the words associated with Katherine's life and career.

W	F	L	F	S	Z	A	L	O	F	A	A	W	A	H	S	Z	A
E	O	U	V	D	U	Y	C	V	Y	Z	N	T	Q	P	W	L	L
S	G	R	D	Y	O	M	R	J	O	H	N	G	L	E	N	N	P
T	P	O	B	N	Z	W	M	N	Z	Y	Y	F	L	E	C	Q	H
V	F	E	T	I	G	W	W	A	J	H	X	R	M	E	N	U	A
I	R	T	S	O	T	I	M	F	C	U	M	A	H	E	H	N	K
R	E	A	F	S	D	A	H	V	M	U	F	L	V	L	A	G	A
G	E	R	F	M	Y	G	L	N	H	F	M	E	F	I	B	K	P
I	D	O	R	A	V	M	Q	M	O	L	L	L	C	Z	Z	Q	P
N	O	T	F	M	T	L	J	L	E	E	N	I	A	I	D	E	A
A	M	C	S	C	V	W	L	K	O	C	T	D	C	U	I	E	A
S	S	O	R	L	V	A	E	L	Y	A	H	Z	V	D	D	C	L
T	E	D	V	A	H	B	L	Z	M	A	T	A	Q	G	Y	E	P
A	V	Q	H	F	W	O	X	E	E	V	N	Y	N	A	S	Q	H
T	E	Z	M	V	P	X	H	Y	S	R	K	J	U	I	J	A	A
E	N	G	F	A	B	T	C	L	B	S	F	W	B	X	C	R	J
H	L	Q	H	Q	A	E	R	B	P	S	P	Q	O	T	K	S	Y
T	T	B	B	M	H	C	N	E	E	R	I	I	O	D	F	Q	O

Find These Words

ORBITALMECHANICS MATHEMATICIAN
HALLOFFAME ALPHAKAPPAALPHA
SUMMACUMLAUDE DOCTORATE
WESTVIRGINASTATE FREEDOMSEVEN
JOHNGLENN APOLLOELEVEN

Directions: Read and answer the questions. These are your opinions so the answers will vary.

Would you rather be famous for an invention or for something you've done?

What's your favorite color?

Share a special memory you have from school.

Directions: Read and answer the questions below. There are clues in the puzzle to help you. Try and solve the cryptic message.

Clue for cryptic message: Katherine worked here.

Questions

1) Katherine was awarded Johnson the _____ Medal of Freedom.

2) Katherine was a member of _____ Kappa Alpha.

3) Katherine was one of the _____ African-American women to work as a NASA scientist.

4) Katherine was inducted into the _____ Women's Hall of Fame.

Directions: This is the WGLT Challenge. Solve the cryptogram. As the puzzle solver, you need to find which number belongs to which character. And this can be pretty challenging! You will need to match the number with the letter. There are some letters given to you below. This will help you solve the other words and unlock more characters. **Good Luck.**

Carter G. Woodson

Carter G. Woodson

December 19, 1875 – April 3, 1950
HISTORIAN

LEFT BLANK ON PURPOSE

Carter G. Woodson

Carter G. Woodson

Carter G. Woodson

Carter G. Woodson

Carter G. Woodson

Carter G. Woodson

Directions: read the bio below and answer the following questions.

Hi, my name is Carter G. Woodson. I was born on December 19, 1875, in New Canton, VA. I graduated from Douglass High School in 1897. In 1900, I was selected to become the principal of Douglass High School. I graduated from Berea College with a bachelor's degree in literature in 1903. From 1903 to 1907, I served as a school supervisor in the Philippines, which had recently become an American territory. I attended the University of Chicago, which is where I earned an A.B. and A.M. in 1908. I was a member of the first Black professional fraternity, Sigma Pi Phi and a member of Omega Psi Phi. I completed my Ph.D. in history at Harvard University in 1912. I founded the Association for the Study of Negro Life and History (ASLNH) in 1915. In January 1916, I began publishing the scholarly Journal of Negro History. In 1926, I celebrated "Negro History Week," which was designated as the second week in February and coincided with the birthdays of Abraham Lincoln and Frederick Douglass.

1. What was my Bachelors Degree in?
    A. History
    B. Science
    C. Literature
2. I wasn't a member of what fraternity?
    A. Sigma Pi Phi
    B. Alpha Phi Alpha
    C. Omega Psi Phi
3. What did I found in 1915?
    A. NAACP
    B. UNIA
    C. ASLNH

Directions: Answer the questions, to solve the crossword puzzle. You can use the internet if you get stuck on any question.

Across

5) Carter taught at historically black colleges _____ and West Virginia State University.

7) Carter was an important figure to the movement of _____.

8) Carter was a member of the first Black _____ fraternity Sigma Pi Phi.

Down

1) Carter began publication of the scholarly Journal of _____ in 1916.

2) Carter was one of the first _____ to study the history of the African diaspora.

3) In 1926, Carter launched the celebration of "Negro _____ Week".

4) Carter going to the 1915's Lincoln _____ inspired him to create the Association for the Study of Negro Life and History (now the Association for the Study of African American Life and History).

6) Carter was a member of ____ Psi Phi.

Directions: Read and answer the questions. These are your opinions so the answers will vary.

Would you rather play an individual or team sport?

_____

_____

What's your favorite genre of book to read?

_____

_____

What goals do you have for yourself? What are 5 things you want to do before you are (21)?

_____

_____

_____

_____

_____

Directions: Unscramble the words below about Carter. See if you can get the bonus word.

BONUS WORD

Unscramble Words

1) ounfred
2) gemiaosphip
3) lhbitntrhasmokyco
4) iaonithrs
5) rtuhao
6) bleereecogal
7) afieairnsmcraacn
8) hiiapipmgs
9) aojlitnsru

Directions: This is the WGLT Challenge. Solve the cryptogram. As the puzzle solver, you need to find which number belongs to which character. And this can be pretty challenging! You will need to match the number with the letter. There are some letters given to you below. This will help you solve the other words and unlock more characters. **Good Luck.**

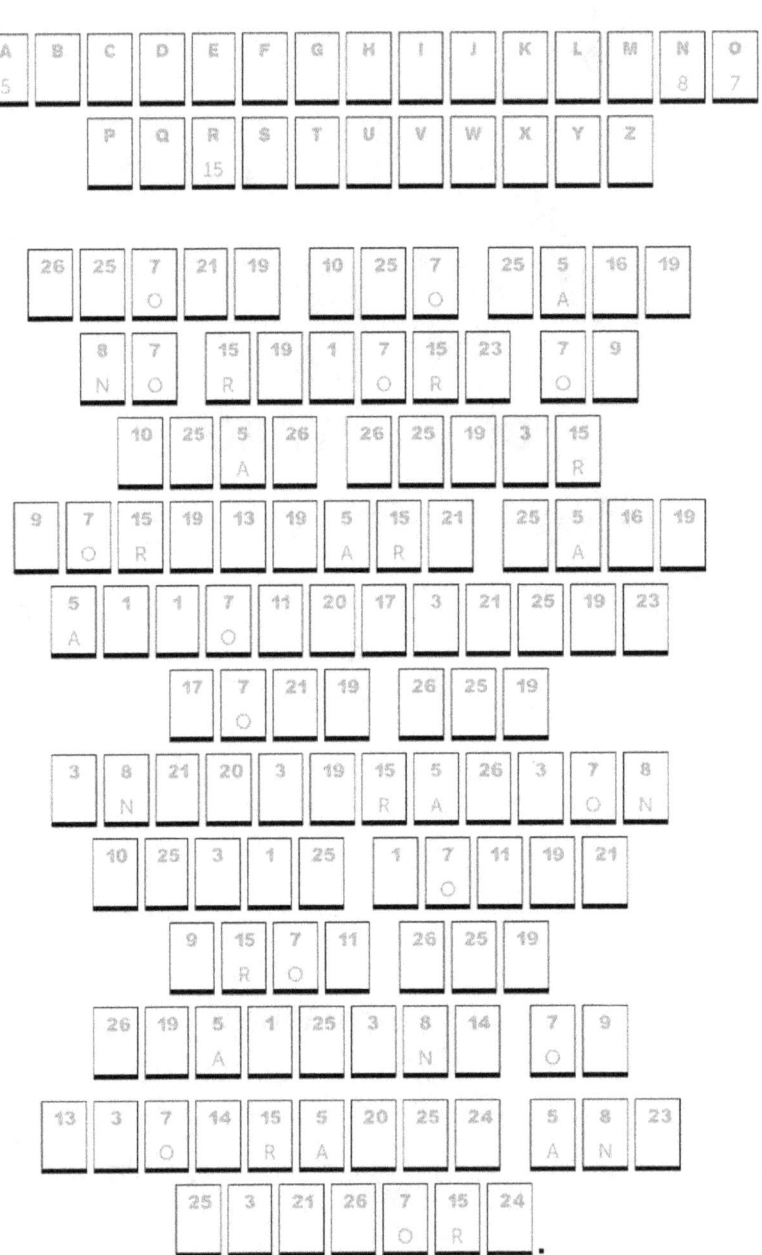

Shonda Rhimes

Shonda Rhimes

January 13, 1970 - PRESENT
TV PRODUCER

LEFT BLANK ON PURPOSE

Shonda Rhimes

Shonda Rhimes

Shonda Rhimes

Shonda Rhimes

Shonda Rhimes

Shonda Rhimes

Directions: read the bio below and answer the following questions.

Hi, my name is Shonda Rhimes. I was born on January 13, 1970, in Chicago, IL. I graduated from Marian Catholic High School. In 1991, I received my bachelor's degree from Dartmouth College in English and film studies. I received a Master of Fine Arts degree from the USC School of Cinematic Arts. While at USC, I was hired as an intern by Debra Martin Chase, who became my mentor. We worked together on The Princess Diaries 2. Some of the things that I have produced at my production company, Shondaland, are Grey's Anatomy (2005-present), Off the Map (2011), Scandal (2012-2018), How to Get Away with Murder (2014-2020), Still Star-Crossed (2017), Station 19 (2018-present) and Bridgerton (2020-present).

1. What college did I get my Masters from?
    A. Dartmouth
    B. University of Chicago
    C. USC
2. What year did Scandal air?
    A. 2012
    B. 2018
    C. 2005
3. What did me and Debra Martin Chase work on?
    A. The Princess Diaries 2
    B. Grey's Anatomy
    C. The Princess Diaries

Directions: Find the words associated with Shonda's life and career.

A	Y	E	G	H	H	T	N	O	T	R	E	G	D	I	R	B	P
M	X	X	W	S	E	C	F	J	K	D	Y	B	R	A	Y	T	R
D	S	E	D	R	A	C	V	I	J	R	P	I	H	Y	S	V	I
A	Q	C	M	H	S	X	C	U	G	R	Z	P	U	S	W	J	V
J	B	U	R	H	Z	T	H	K	O	H	P	Z	N	H	G	Y	A
F	T	T	O	E	D	F	H	D	C	S	E	9	Q	O	C	G	T
U	T	I	H	W	V	O	U	T	Y	T	1	F	Z	W	D	T	E
X	X	V	T	D	U	C	A	B	M	N	Q	V	D	R	A	S	P
B	U	E	U	A	E	C	C	H	O	P	F	S	T	U	T	I	R
H	Z	P	A	R	E	F	I	I	C	K	Q	D	Q	N	H	N	A
G	M	R	F	H	B	K	T	K	H	Z	P	V	N	N	E	Y	C
P	X	O	T	G	Y	A	F	R	B	K	N	T	W	E	N	K	T
D	G	D	Z	G	T	N	J	P	C	U	F	L	R	R	K	O	I
K	D	U	Z	S	R	J	V	P	Z	R	E	Z	O	D	X	U	C
M	Z	C	Y	S	C	R	E	E	N	W	R	I	T	E	R	O	E
H	E	E	W	S	O	K	L	H	L	K	J	A	Z	R	L	C	N
I	M	R	S	U	Q	W	B	I	G	G	R	E	E	N	W	C	Y
E	A	I	A	J	P	T	D	Z	X	T	X	Z	V	E	M	P	Z

Find These Words

BIGGREEN SCREENWRITER THECATCH
PRODUCER PRIVATEPRACTICE AUTHOR
SHOWRUNNER EXECUTIVEPRODUCER BRIDGERTON
STATION19

Directions: Read and answer the questions. These are your opinions so the answers will vary.

Would you rather text your friends or get together?

What's your favorite story about your life so far?

Describe a situation where you showed extra kindness toward a stranger/friend.

Directions: Read and answer the questions below. There are clues in the puzzle to help you. Try and solve the cryptic message.

Clue for cryptic message: This was one of Shonda's shows.

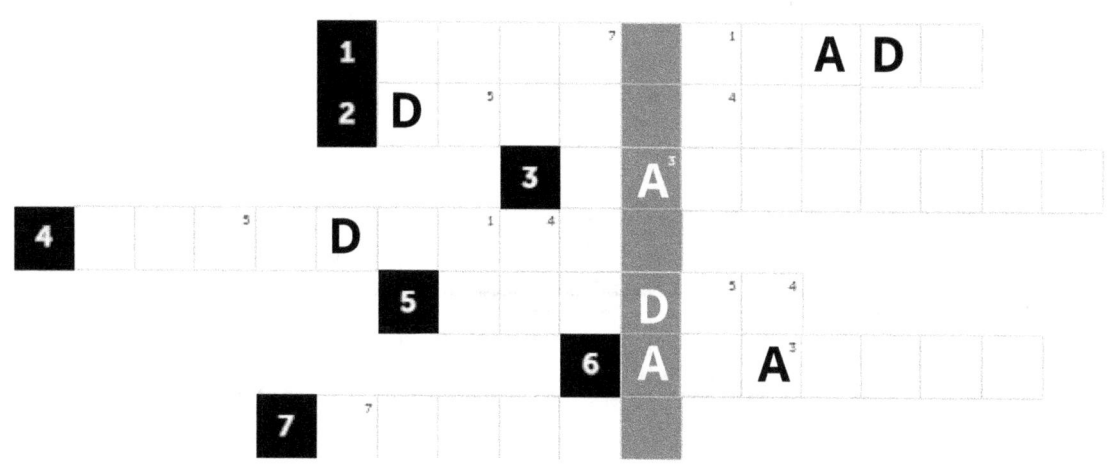

Questions

1) Shonda first film was "_____," starring Britney Spears.

2) Shonda made a short film, Blossoms and Veils, which is her only credit as a film ____.

3) Shonda graduated from _____ College.

4) Shonda's first show from her Netflix deal was "_____".

5) Shonda first real screenwriting ____ was the HBO TV film "Introducing Dorothy Dandridge," with Halle Berry.

6) Shonda is best known for creating the hugely successful, "Grey's ____."

7) Shonda wrote "The Princess Diaries 2: Royal Engagement," the 2004 _____ to Disney's popular 2001 movie "The Princess Diaries."

Directions: This is the WGLT Challenge. Solve the cryptogram. As the puzzle solver, you need to find which number belongs to which character. And this can be pretty challenging! You will need to match the number with the letter. There are some letters given to you below. This will help you solve the other words and unlock more characters. **Good Luck.**

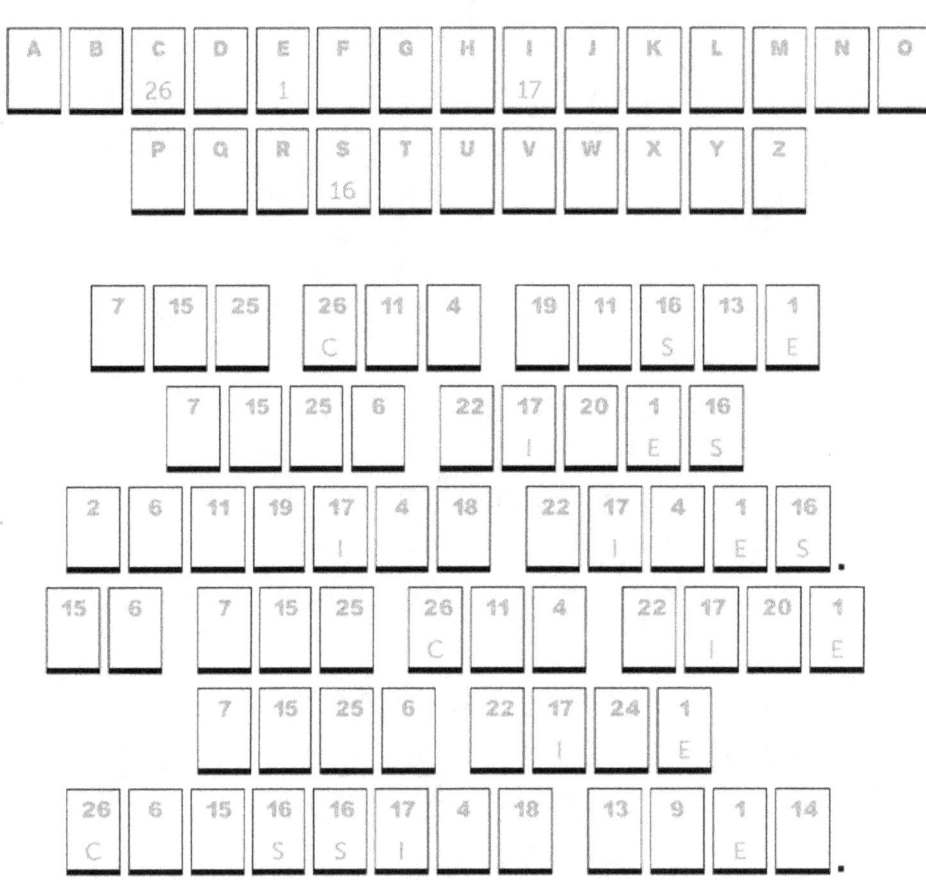

Michael Wilbon

Michael Wilbon

November 19, 1958 - PRESENT
COMMENTATOR **115**

LEFT BLANK ON PURPOSE

Michael Wilbon

Michael Wilbon

Michael Wilbon

Michael Wilbon

Michael Wilbon

Michael Wilbon

Directions: read the bio below and answer the following questions.

Hi, my name is Michael Wilbon. I was born on November 19, 1958, in Chicago, IL. I graduated from St. Ignatius College Preparatory School in 1976. I received my journalism degree in 1980 from Northwestern University's Medill School of Journalism. I wrote for The Daily Northwestern in college. In 1980, I started working for The Washington Post and I covered college sports, Major League Baseball, the National Football League and the National Basketball Association up to four times a week until I left to work full-time for ESPN in 2010. I have covered ten Summer and Winter Olympic Games for The Washington Post, every Super Bowl since 1987, nearly every Final Four since 1982 and each year's NBA Finals since 1987. In 2001, I started co-hosting ESPN's daily opinion forum Pardon the Interruption (PTI).

1. What was the name of the college I went to?
   A. University of Chicago
   B. Illinois University
   C. Northwestern University
2. What year did I start working for ESPN?
   A. 2005
   B. 2010
   C. 2011
3. How many Olympic games have I covered?
   A. 12
   B. 9
   C. 10

118

Directions: Answer the questions, to solve the crossword puzzle. You can use the internet if you get stuck on any question.

Across

1) Michael is an analyst for ESPN and has co-hosted _____ the Interruption.
3) Michael has covered ten _____ and Winter Olympic Games.
5) Michael started working for The _____ in 1980.
6) Michael wrote his last _____ for the Washington Post in 2010.
7) Michael is a member of ABC's NBA _____.

Down

1) Michael is considered to be a TV _____.
2) Michael was _____ into the Northwestern University Athletic Hall of Fame.
4) Michael covered _____ sports, Major League Baseball, the National Football League and the National Basketball Association.

Directions: Read and answer the questions. These are your opinions so the answers will vary.

Would you rather be a wizard or a superhero?

What's your favorite video game?

Why do you think it is important to have rules in school?

Directions: Unscramble the words below about Michael. See if you can get the bonus word.

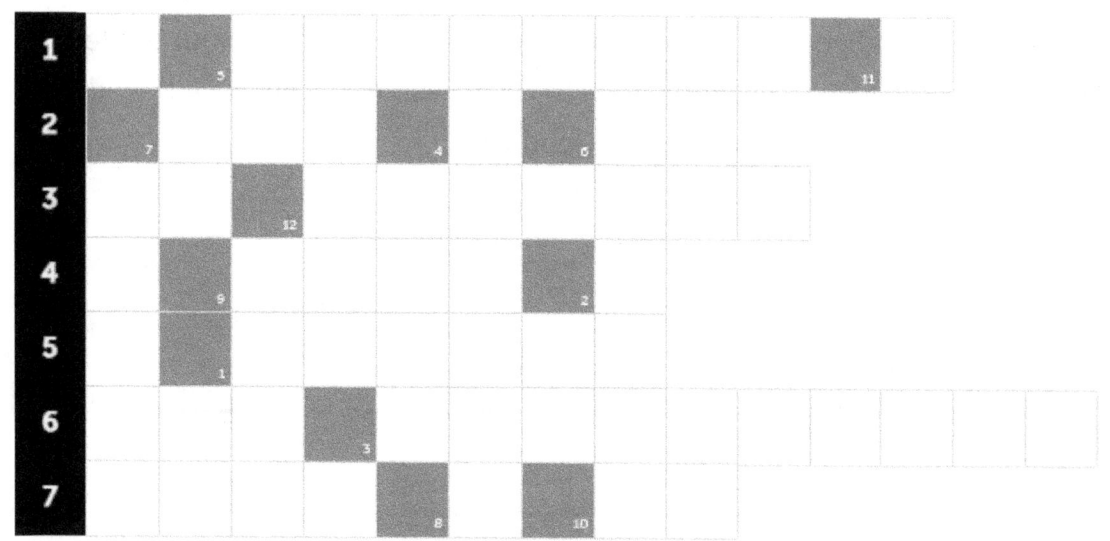

BONUS WORD

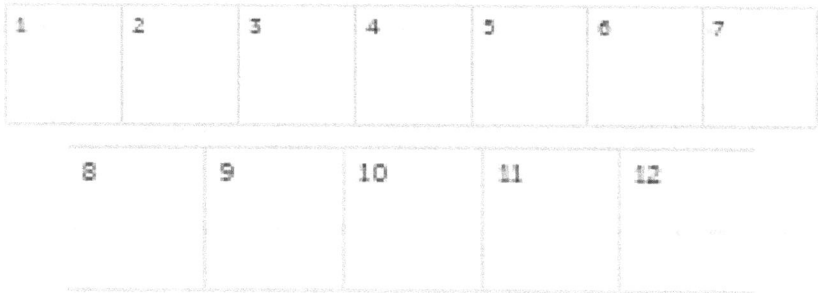

Unscramble Words

1) rsitpowrsetr
2) nctomlsui
3) ekbtblsaal
4) ablabels
5) foboallt
6) korosihrnyente
7) boemslagw

121

Directions: This is the WGLT Challenge. Solve the cryptogram. As the puzzle solver, you need to find which number belongs to which character. And this can be pretty challenging! You will need to match the number with the letter. There are some letters given to you below. This will help you solve the other words and unlock more characters. **Good Luck.**

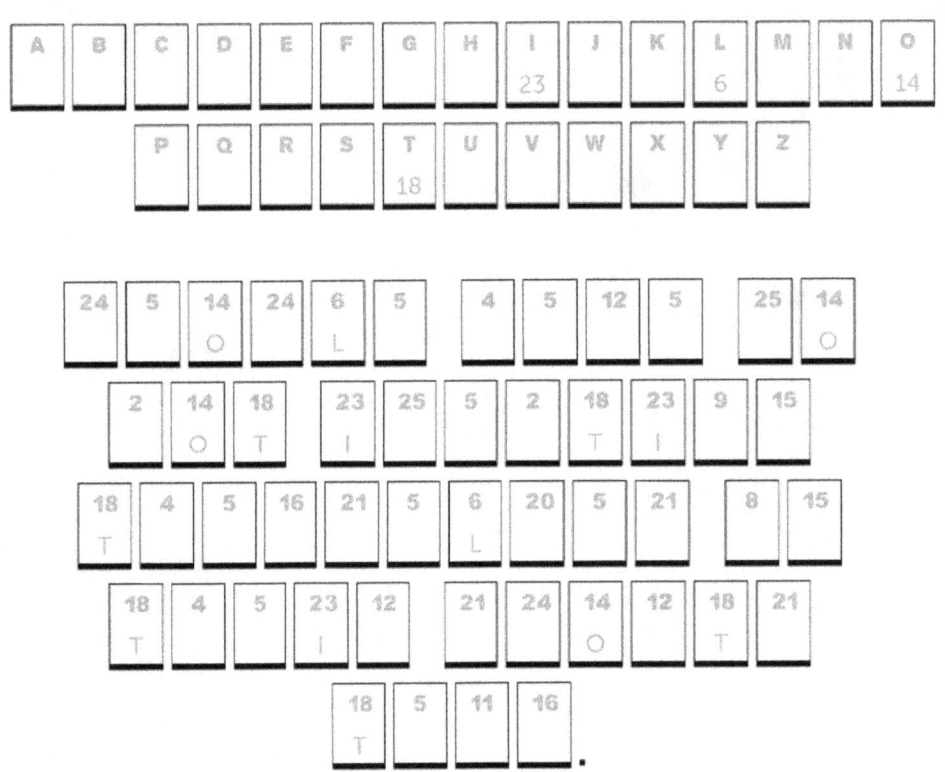

Rebecca Crumpler

Rebecca Crumpler

February 8, 1831 – March 9, 1895
PHYSICIAN

LEFT BLANK ON PURPOSE

Rebecca Crumpler

Rebecca Crumpler

Rebecca Crumpler

Rebecca Crumpler

Rebecca Crumpler

Rebecca Crumpler

Directions: read the bio below and answer the following questions.

Hi, my name is Rebecca Davis. I was born on February 8, 1831, in Christiana, DE. I earned a place at the New England Female Medical College (NEFMC) in 1860. The school was the first in the country to train women M.D.s. Most medical schools barred Black students regardless of gender. I graduated from New England Female Medical College after having completed three years of coursework, a thesis and final oral examinations in February 1864. On March 1, 1864, the board of trustees named me a doctor of medicine. I became the first African American woman to become a doctor of medicine in the United States. I also was one of the first female physician authors in the nineteenth century. In 1883, I published Book of Medical Discourses. I first practiced medicine in Boston. I primarily cared for poor African American women and children. I also worked for the Freedmen's Bureau to provide medical care to freed slaves who were denied care by white physicians.

1. What college did I graduate from?
    A. New England Female Medical College
    B. Chicago Medical College
    C. Northwestern University School of Medicine
2. What was the name of my book?
    A. Medical Mysteries
    B. Medicine from a Doctor point of view
    C. Book of Medical Discourses
3. I was the first African American woman in the U.S. to?
    A. Become a Nurse
    B. Become a Doctor
    C. Become a Teacher

Directions: Find the words associated with Rebecca's life and career.

```
A T X Y W Y O W E E Q G U Z D B X C
T H N O D S F Z R Y R I L X Y U N V
J Z M S A M U E L G R E G O R Y F M
E E U V D N A L G N E W E N T M X B
C B O A K C O T T X B C R N D Y K G
S P F I E F R E E S L A V E S N Y P
B H V R G R N K Q D L U B T C C N Z
G Y F U P L J O J R L A I T K O R
Q S V C U A Y B L N I S V N X S T O
Y I R O T C O D S L A I O Q Q F G H
Q C V B A U K F N N L V H X C B N T
V I F E B J L K Y W E T H I A V I U
Q A N O T S O B A M O M X A C F M A
E N Y D D L V R M D S F D J J K L V
R U U D U V D R O M I J X E R T I H
C P L U P Q F K U L B I Y T E X W M
E G R T Z X Z M V F R A I G E R Y N
F A M F F U G Q L R I C N K Z J F S
```

Find These Words

NEWENGLAND   PHYSICIAN   CIVILWAR
FREFSLAVES   DOCTOR   FREEDMENSBUREAU
BOSTON   AUTHOR   SAMUELGREGORY
WILMINGTON

127

Directions: Read and answer the questions. These are your opinions so the answers will vary.

Would you rather play hide-and-seek or dodgeball?

What's your favorite subject in school?

What is one rule in all schools that you feel is unfair?

Directions: Read and answer the questions below. There are clues in the puzzle to help you. Try and solve the cryptic message.

Clue for cryptic message: Rebecca became one of these.

Questions

1) Rebecca was able to study medicine due to the heavy demands of _____ care for Civil War veterans.

2) Rebecca studied at the New England Female Medical _____.

3) Rebecca was one of the first female _____ authors during that time.

4) Rebecca's home is part of the Boston Women's _____ Trail.

5) Rebecca was the first African-American woman to become a _____ of medicine in the United States.

6) Rebecca worked for the Freedmen's Bureau to provide medical care for _____ slaves.

Directions: This is the WGLT Challenge. Solve the cryptogram. As the puzzle solver, you need to find which number belongs to which character. And this can be pretty challenging! You will need to match the number with the letter. There are some letters given to you below. This will help you solve the other words and unlock more characters. **Good Luck.**

130

Stephen A. Smith

Stephen A. Smith

131

October 14, 1967 - PRESENT
SPORTS TELEVISION PERSONALITY

LEFT BLANK ON PURPOSE

Stephen A. Smith

Stephen A. Smith

Stephen A. Smith

Stephen A. Smith

Stephen A. Smith

Stephen A. Smith

Directions: read the bio below and answer the following questions.

Hi, my name is Stephen Anthony Smith. I was born on October 14, 1967, in the Bronx, NY. I graduated from Thomas Edison High School. In 1991, I graduated from Winston-Salem State University with a Bachelor of Arts in Mass Communication. I'm also a member of the Omega Psi Phi fraternity. In 1994, I had a position as a writer for The Philadelphia Inquirer. I reported on the Philadelphia 76ers as their NBA columnist and eventually sports in general. In 2005, I became the host of a weekday noon-to-2 p.m. radio show on WEPN in New York City. In 2009, I became an on-air contributor to Fox Sports Radio and broke the story of Allen Iverson's retirement on the Chris Myers and Steve Hartman afternoon show on November 25. Iverson later ended his short retirement and re-joined the Philadelphia 76ers on December 2. I became a Fox Sports Radio morning show host on January 4, 2010.

1. What is my Bachelors Degree in?
    A. Sports Medicine
    B. Mass Communication
    C. Journalism
2. What HBCU did I graduate from?
    A. Winston-Salem State University
    B. Fisk University
    C. Howard University
3. What fraternity am I a member of?
    A. Alpha Phi Alpha
    B. Kappa Alpha Psi
    C. Omega Psi Phi

Directions: Answer the questions, to solve the crossword puzzle. You can use the internet if you get stuck on any question.

Across
3) Stephen debuted on radio in 2005 on _____ city's station 'WEPN-FM'
4) Stephen worked for the sports columnist for the _____ Inquirer.
5) Stephen became a member of the _____ Psi Phi fraternity.
6) Stephen had his own show with ESPN called '_____ Frankly with Stephen A. Smith.'
7) Stephen went to the Fashion Institute of _____ for only one year.
8) Stephen got a _____ scholarship to attend Winston-Salem State University.

Down
1) Stephen correctly _____ that LeBron James, Dwyane Wade and Chris Bosh would all sign with the Miami Heat during 2010 free agency.
2) Stephen made his acting debut on the ABC _____ General Hospital in a cameo appearance as a television reporter.

135

Directions: Read and answer the questions. These are your opinions so the answers will vary.

Would you rather eat at home or in a restaurant?

What's your favorite activity to do with friends?

Do peers deserve the same respect as elders? Why?

Directions: Unscramble the words below about Stephen. See if you can get the bonus word.

BONUS WORD

1	2	3	4	5	6

7	8	9	10	11	12	13	14	15	16	17

Unscramble Words

1) taetsopvyrnil   **2)** rtsfkaeit   **3)** enps
4) acoeomtrmnt   **5)** nihledirhlirpauqpeai   **6)** nm-osiwteslan
7) noorergbse   **8)** leblsbaakt

137

Directions: This is the WGLT Challenge. Solve the cryptogram. As the puzzle solver, you need to find which number belongs to which character. And this can be pretty challenging! You will need to match the number with the letter. There are some letters given to you below. This will help you solve the other words and unlock more characters. **Good Luck.**

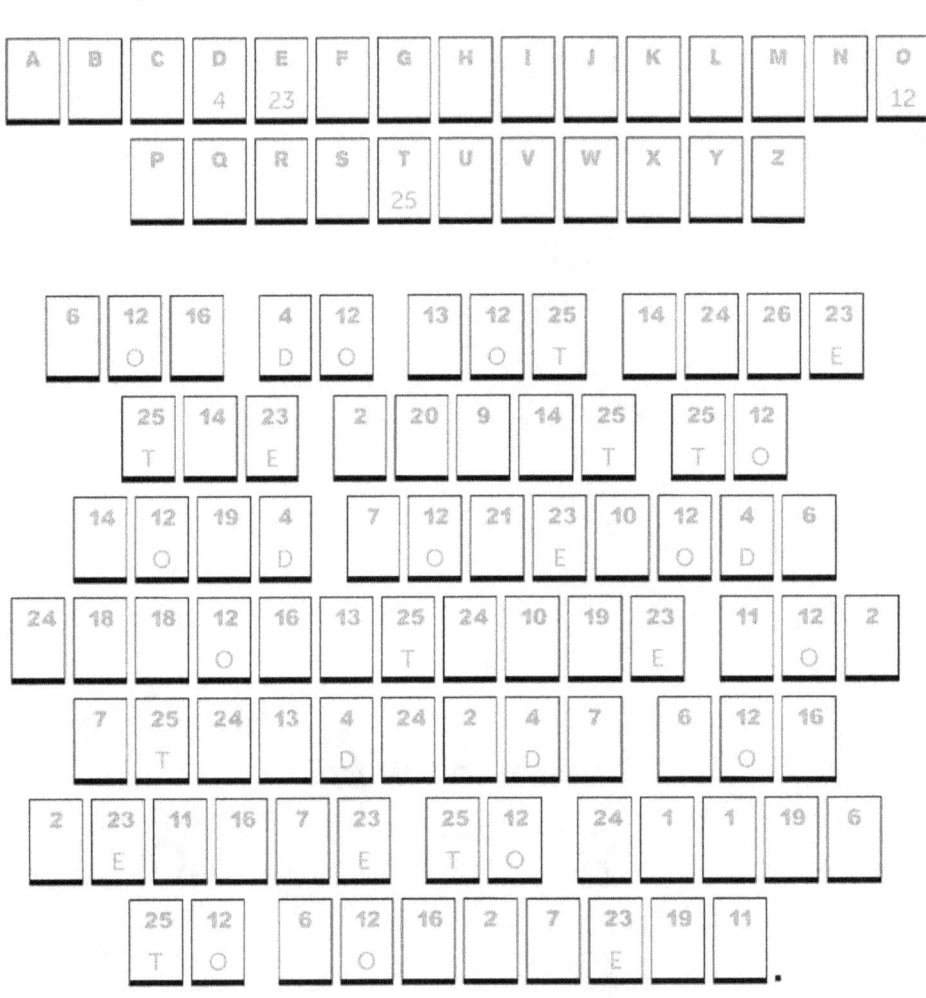

Ida Bell Wells-Barnet

Ida Bell Wells-Barnet

July 16, 1862 – March 25, 1931
INVESTIGATIVE JOURNALIST

LEFT BLANK ON PURPOSE

Ida Bell Wells-Barnet

Ida Bell Wells-Barnet

Ida Bell Wells-Barnet

Ida Bell Wells-Barnet

Ida Bell Wells-Barnet

Ida Bell Wells-Barnet

Directions: read the bio below and answer the following questions.

Hi, my name is Ida Bell Wells. I was born on July 16, 1862, in Holly Springs, MS. I attended Lemoyne-Owen College, Rust College and Fisk University. In 1883, I moved to Memphis and started working for the Shelby County school system. I also took an editorial position for a small Memphis journal, the Evening Star and I began writing weekly articles for The Living Way newspaper under the pen name "Lola." My focus at the time under my pen name was to attack racist Jim Crow policies. In 1889, I became the editor and co-owner with J. L. Fleming of The Free Speech and Headlight. This was a Black-owned newspaper that was established by Rev. Taylor Nightingale (1844–1922). In 1892, my Free Speech office was destroyed, which included my articles about the poor conditions for Black-only Memphis schools and the unlawful lynching that was going on. In 1892, I had to move to NY. I accepted a job with New York Age and published my research on lynching in a pamphlet titled Southern Horrors: Lynch Law in All Its Phases.

1. What was the city I work for in 1883?
    A. Tennessee
    B. Memphis
    C. Holly Springs
2. What year did I become editor of The Free Sprech?
    A. 1889
    B. 1892
    C. 1890
3. What was my pen name?
    A. Lizzie
    B. Bella
    C. Lola

Directions: Find the words associated with Ida's life and career.

I	E	C	M	T	S	I	L	A	N	R	U	O	J	N	U	G	M
Q	B	B	R	K	A	E	H	I	E	V	Y	V	C	M	L	W	S
G	F	M	S	V	J	S	I	H	P	M	E	M	L	B	W	Q	G
U	J	E	T	G	X	Z	Z	E	G	N	T	E	O	L	L	T	M
S	D	V	R	T	U	W	W	S	Q	W	C	Y	G	W	Y	H	K
Q	H	S	G	H	Y	O	D	O	E	R	O	T	A	X	N	E	W
Z	C	T	V	U	U	E	F	D	E	O	E	Y	C	Y	C	L	F
C	V	H	O	Y	B	X	L	I	R	A	A	F	I	X	H	N	X
E	M	G	J	M	A	Q	S	L	C	E	C	O	H	W	I	L	C
O	H	I	R	W	G	W	D	H	O	P	K	Z	C	E	N	Z	J
N	E	R	Y	T	I	R	I	G	R	W	G	A	J	W	G	J	Z
Q	R	L	E	P	D	N	N	V	X	S	F	Y	E	G	A	B	V
T	P	I	Y	X	G	U	G	A	L	C	M	E	S	P	R	Q	T
G	J	V	O	A	C	J	K	H	A	M	J	D	V	B	S	L	V
C	P	I	P	B	M	F	U	Q	V	C	B	P	S	E	E	Y	T
Q	Q	C	T	P	C	C	V	E	G	O	P	Z	I	M	R	N	Z
V	C	B	P	E	Z	I	R	P	R	E	Z	T	I	L	U	P	S
Z	B	N	C	C	T	I	B	A	G	Q	S	P	T	M	M	Z	K

Find These Words

TEACHING   CHICAGO   CIVILRIGHTS
MEMPHIS   JOURNALIST   NAACP
YELLOWFEVER   SPEAKER   LYNCHING
PULITZERPRIZE

Directions: Read and answer the questions. These are your opinions so the answers will vary.

Would you rather visit the mountains or the ocean?

What's your favorite show on TV?

How do you prefer others show kindness- hugs, notes, time together, etc?

Directions: Read and answer the questions below. There are clues in the puzzle to help you. Try and solve the cryptic message.

Clue for cryptic message: Ida spoke up about this.

Questions

1) Ida raised her ____ after both of their parents died from yellow fever.

2) Ida started writing a new column called 'The Living ____.'

3) Ida sued a railroad company for _____ and won, but lost on an appeal due to Jim Crow laws.

4) Ida's Alpha Suffrage Club were instrumental in getting ____ De Priest elected to the U.S. House of Representatives.

5) Ida started _____ right after her parents passed away.

6) Ida was born into slavery, but was freed be the _____ Proclamation.

7) Ida was one of the _____ of the National Association for the Advancement of Colored People (NAACP).

8) Ida founded the Alpha ____ Club of Chicago.

Directions: This is the WGLT Challenge. Solve the cryptogram. As the puzzle solver, you need to find which number belongs to which character. And this can be pretty challenging! You will need to match the number with the letter. There are some letters given to you below. This will help you solve the other words and unlock more characters. **Good Luck.**

147

July 10, 1875 – May 18, 1955
EDUCATOR

LEFT BLANK ON PURPOSE

Mary Mcleod Bethune

Mary Mcleod Bethune

Mary Mcleod Bethune

Mary Mcleod Bethune

Mary Mcleod Bethune

Mary Mcleod Bethune

Directions: read the bio below and answer the following questions.

Hi, my name is Mary Jane McLeod. I was born on July 10, 1875, in Mayesville, SC. I attended Trinity Mission School. I was the only child in my family to attend school. In 1888, I attended Scotia Seminary (which is now Barber-Scotia College). I moved to Florida in 1899, where I ran the mission school and began an outreach to prisoners. In 1904, I opened a school in Florida. It cost $1.50 to start the Educational and Industrial Training School for Negro Girls. I received a donation of $62,000 from John D. Rockefeller. My friendship with Franklin D. Roosevelt and his wife granted me entry to a progressive network. In 1931, the Methodist Church helped my school merge with the boys' Cookman Institute, which became Bethune-Cookman College, which was a coeducational junior college. I continued to operate the college and met the educational standards of the State of Florida. In 1941, the college had developed a four-year curriculum and achieved full college status. Our school's library became Florida's first free library that was accessible to Black Floridians.

1. What was the name of the school I started?
   A. Bethune-Cookman College
   B. Educational and Industrial Training School
   C. Cookman College
2. Bethune-Cookman College achieve full college status in?
   A. 1931
   B. 1904
   C. 1941
3. What state is Bethune-Cookman College in?
   A. South Carolina
   B. North Carolina
   C. Florida

Directions: Answer the questions, to solve the crossword puzzle. You can use the internet if you get stuck on any question.

Across

1) The U.S. _____ honored Mary by having her picture on a stamp.
3) Mary was named to the National Women's _____.
6) Mary was a close friend of Eleanor _____.
7) Mary was an adviser to several American _____.
8) Mary wanted to be a _____ in Africa, but at the time African Americans were not allowed to do this.

Down

2) Mary received a _____ to attend Scotia Seminary, a school for African American girls.
4) Franklin D. Roosevelt _____ Mary director of African American affairs in the National Youth Administration.
5) Mary established a school for African American girls in Daytona Beach, ___.

Directions: Read and answer the questions. These are your opinions so the answers will vary.

Would you rather have art or PE?

What's your favorite activity to do with family?

Why do you think it is important to have rules in society?

Directions: Unscramble the words below about Mary. See if you can get the bonus word.

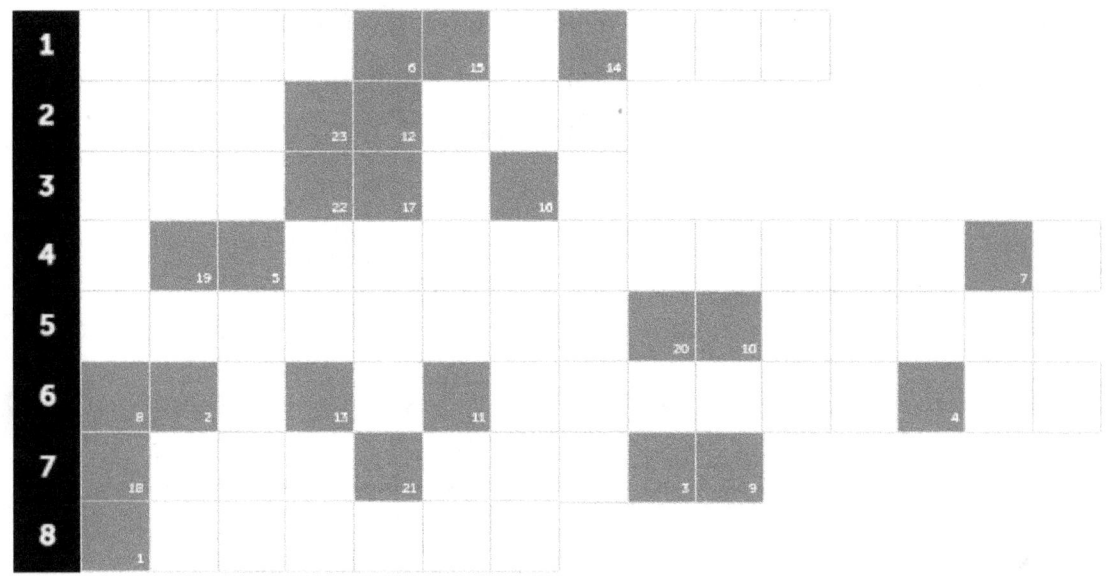

BONUS WORD

Unscramble Words

1) igitlvihscr
2) onitmsaw
3) aertucdo
4) onomt-kehuebnac
5) ihptliatrsohnp
6) aiednsecrnidhfs
7) oinmayssir
8) orfliad

153

Directions: This is the WGLT Challenge. Solve the cryptogram. As the puzzle solver, you need to find which number belongs to which character. And this can be pretty challenging! You will need to match the number with the letter. There are some letters given to you below. This will help you solve the other words and unlock more characters. **Good Luck.**

154

Alexa Irene Canady

Alexa Irene Canady

November 7, 1950 - PRESENT
PEDIATRIC NEUROSURGERY

LEFT BLANK ON PURPOSE

Alexa Irene Canady

Alexa Irene Canady

Alexa Irene Canady

Alexa Irene Canady

Alexa Irene Canady

Alexa Irene Canady

Directions: read the bio below and answer the following questions.

Hi, my name is Alexa Canady. I was born on November 7, 1950, in Lansing, MI. In 1967, I graduated with honors from Lansing Sexton High School. In 1971, I received my Bachelor of Science in Zoology from the University of Michigan. I also became a member of the Delta Sigma Theta sorority. In 1975, I earned my M.D. with cum laude honors from the University of Michigan Medical School. I'm also a member of the Alpha Omega Alpha Honorary Medical Society. In 1975, I became a surgical intern at the Yale New Haven Hospital and became the first Black and female intern in the program. I went to the University of Minnesota for my residency and became the first female African American neurosurgery resident in the United States. In 1982, after finishing my residency, I specialized as a pediatric neurosurgeon, which made me the first African American and the first woman to do so. In 1984, I became the first African American woman to be a board-certified neurosurgeon.

1. What sorority am I a member of?
   A. Alpha Kappa Alpha
   B. Zeta Phi Beta
   C. Delta Sigma Theta
2. What college did I get my B.S. degree from?
   A. University of Michigan State
   B. University of Michigan
   C. University of Minnesota
3. I was the first African-American woman to be?
   A. Board-certified Neurosurgeon
   B. Board-certified Doctor
   C. Board-certified Physician

Directions: Find the words associated with Alexa's life and career.

C	B	R	Q	D	Y	M	Q	A	B	V	S	T	D	Z	W	S	P
H	E	G	S	B	M	F	C	M	Z	E	U	E	M	O	J	B	I
I	Z	S	B	C	F	E	G	Y	W	E	N	S	L	O	P	L	U
L	B	R	R	A	Y	M	W	N	W	O	I	P	E	L	U	X	J
D	E	O	A	S	S	R	O	E	F	I	E	V	C	O	X	D	A
R	M	T	I	U	U	L	E	Q	V	D	B	P	Q	G	F	Z	M
E	A	C	N	Z	W	L	R	G	I	F	F	S	W	Y	K	A	M
N	F	O	T	E	I	Y	A	A	R	Z	O	Y	F	T	S	B	E
S	F	D	U	Z	K	M	T	H	W	U	H	K	J	U	A	E	Q
H	O	L	M	N	M	R	R	P	T	S	C	K	O	O	M	Z
O	L	A	O	H	I	W	D	K	V	E	D	O	T	S	I	U	E
S	L	C	R	C	T	H	H	V	J	E	C	R	R	C	R	O	W
P	A	I	S	N	P	T	R	F	T	R	M	O	H	U	D	L	V
I	H	D	J	W	J	D	K	X	U	Z	C	I	R	I	E	L	M
T	S	E	V	T	Y	P	Y	W	S	S	G	X	Z	D	A	N	W
A	P	M	M	P	A	P	W	V	L	A	A	C	V	C	Y	W	V
L	J	N	Q	F	P	I	C	O	N	W	C	C	L	T	U	H	D
B	O	A	R	D	-	C	E	R	T	I	F	I	E	D	N	B	E

Find these words

PEDIATRIC MICHIGAN NEUROSURGERY
MEDICALDOCTOR BRAINTUMORS ZOOLOGY
CHILDRENSHOSPITAL BOARD-CERTIFIED HYDROCEPHALUS
HALLOFFAME

Directions: Read and answer the questions. These are your opinions so the answers will vary.

If you could travel anywhere in our solar system, where would you go?

What's your favorite meal of the day?

Have you volunteered in your community?

Directions: Read and answer the questions below. There are clues in the puzzle to help you. Try and solve the cryptic message.

Clue for cryptic message: Alexa was born here.

Questions

1) Alexa got her Bachelor's degree in _____ from the University of Michigan.
2) Alexa is a member of Delta _____ Theta.
3) Alexa was inducted into the ____ Women's Hall of Fame.
4) Alexa was the first African-American to _____ as a pediatric neurosurgeon.
5) Alexa is a member of the Alpha Omega Alpha Honorary _____ Society.
6) Alexa was _____ as a National Achievement Scholar.
7) Alexa became the first black woman to become a _____.

Directions: This is the WGLT Challenge. Solve the cryptogram. As the puzzle solver, you need to find which number belongs to which character. And this can be pretty challenging! You will need to match the number with the letter. There are some letters given to you below. This will help you solve the other words and unlock more characters. **Good Luck.**

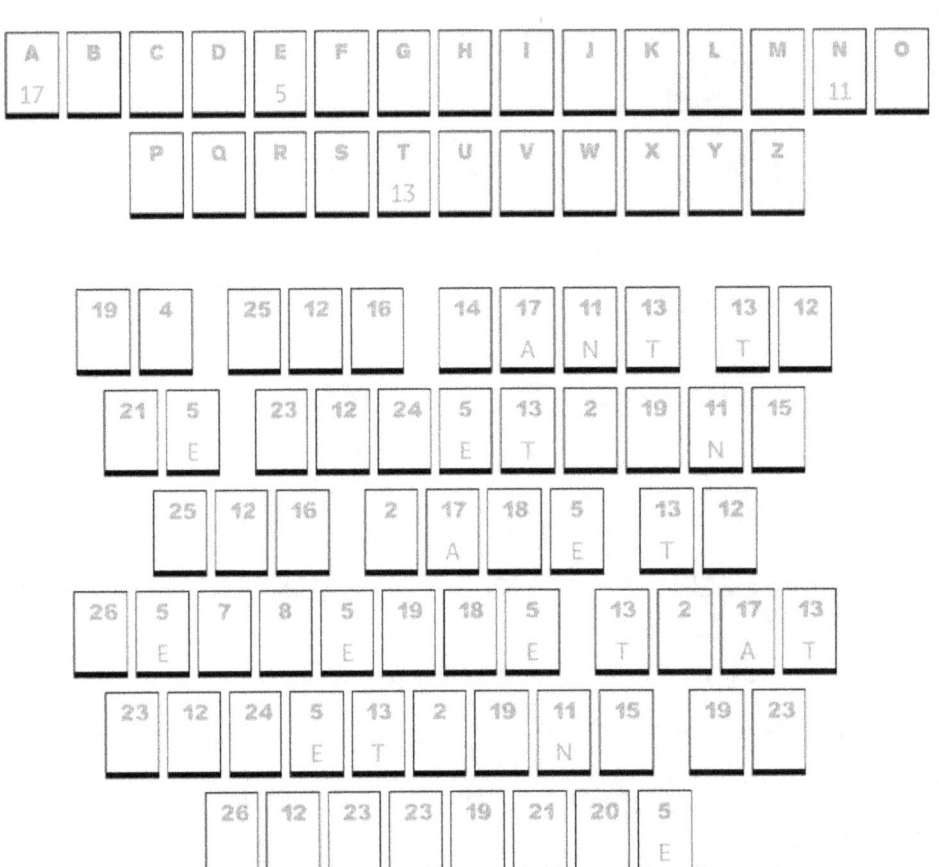

162

Fern Hunt

Fern Hunt

JANUARY 14, 1948 - PRESENT
MATHEMATICIAN

163

Fern Hunt

Fern Hunt

Fern Hunt

Fern Hunt

Fern Hunt

Fern Hunt

Directions: read the bio below and answer the following questions.

Hi, my name is Mary Y. Hunt. I was born in March 1822 in New York City, NY. I graduated from Bronx High School of Science. I graduated with a bachelor's degree in mathematics from Bryn Mawr College in 1969. I received my master's degree and Ph.D. in mathematics from the Courant Institute of Mathematics at New York University in 1978. I worked for Howard University's Mathematics Department as an associate professor in 1978. In 1981, I worked in the mathematical biology laboratory at the National Institute of Health (NIH). In 1993, I started my career at the National Institute of Standards and Technology (NIST) in the computing and applied mathematics laboratory. I give lectures at colleges and universities to encourage students to pursue mathematics.

1. What college did I get my Ph. D from?
   A. New York City University
   B. New York University
   C. State University of New York
2. What year did I start working for NIST?
   A. 1978
   B. 1993
   C. 1981
3. What do I encourage students to do?
   A. medical
   B. mathematics
   C. cooking

Directions: Answer the questions, to solve the crossword puzzle. You can use the internet if you get stuck on any question.

Across

3) Fern research interests include dynamical systems and applied _____.
6) Fern decided to pursue mathematics when she was _____ years old.
7) Fern's family is originally from _____.
8) Fern received both her M.S. and Ph.D. degrees from the _____.

Down

1) Fern has been an active _____ in the Conference of African American Researchers in the Mathematical Sciences (CAARMS).
2) Fern worked as an associate professor at Howard University's _____ Department.
4) Fern was a member of the _____ Record Examination Mathematics Advisory Board.
5) Fern worked for the National Institutes of _____ in the Laboratory of Mathematical Biology.

Directions: Read and answer the questions. These are your opinions so the answers will vary.

If you could meet a musician or group, who would it be?

What's your favorite subject to learn about in school?

In your free time, what do you like to do?

Directions: Unscramble the words below about Mary. See if you can get the bonus word.

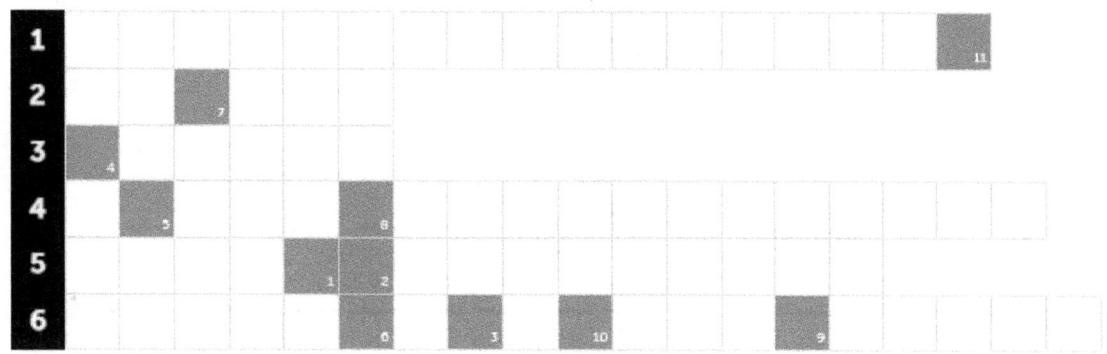

BONUS WORD

Unscramble Words
1) cedelaapaitispmmt
2) thhale
3) waohrd
4) drnatetmfeeyroegnp
5) egrrnlewbyamolc
6) ogiylabtheaoacmlmit

Directions: This is the WGLT Challenge. Solve the cryptogram. As the puzzle solver, you need to find which number belongs to which character. And this can be pretty challenging! You will need to match the number with the letter. There are some letters given to you below. This will help you solve the other words and unlock more characters. **Good Luck.**

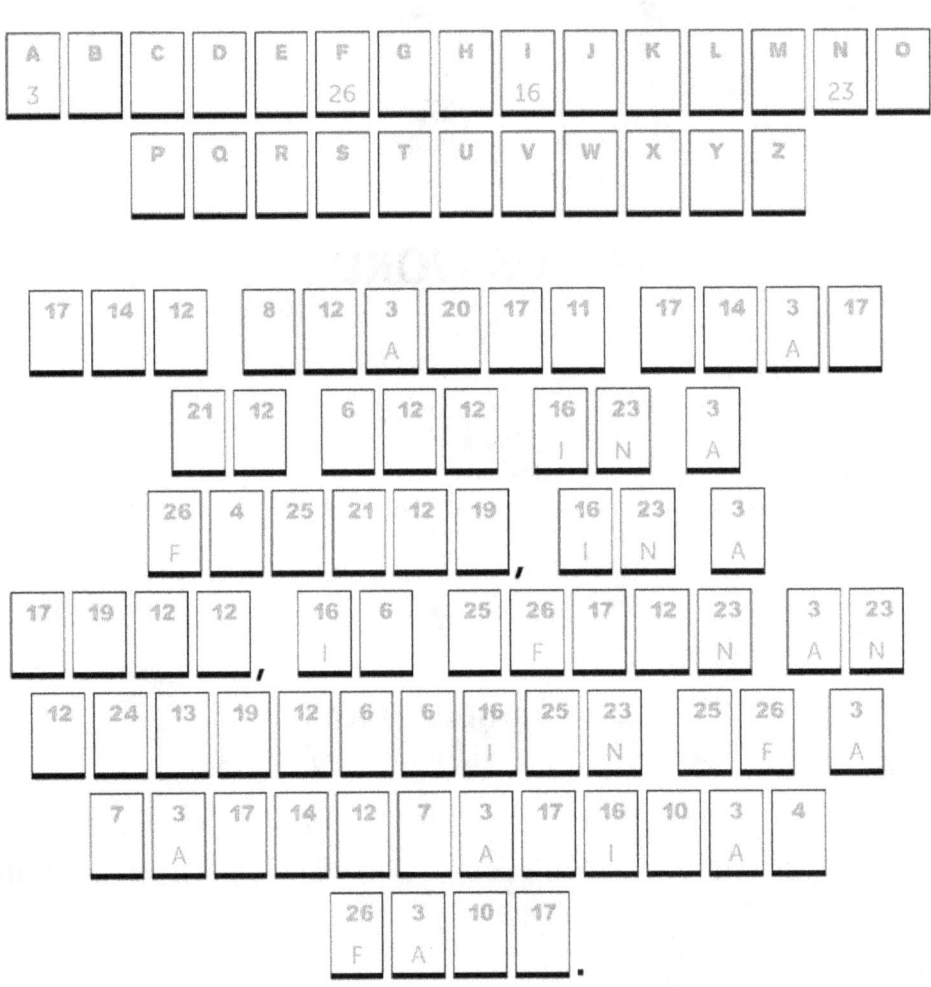

Ketanji Brown Jackson

Ketanji Brown Jackson

March 1822 – March 10, 1913
ABOLITIONIST

171

Ketanji Brown Jackson

Ketanji Brown Jackson

Ketanji Brown Jackson

Ketanji Brown Jackson

Ketanji Brown Jackson

Ketanji Brown Jackson

Directions: read the bio below and answer the following questions.

Hi, my name is Ketanji Onyika Brown. I was born on September 14, 1970, in Washington, D.C. I graduated from Miami Palmetto Senior High School in 1988. In 1992, I graduated magna cum laude from Harvard University with a Bachelor of Arts. In 1996, I graduated cum laude from Harvard with a Juris Doctor degree. I served as a law clerk for judge Patti B. Saris of the U.S. District Court for the District of Massachusetts in 1996, then for judge Bruce M. Selya of the United States Court of Appeals for the First Circuit in 1997. I clerked for U.S. Supreme Court Justice Stephen Breyer from 1999 to 2000. I was confirmed by the full Senate in 2013 to serve as a judge for the United States District Court for the District of Columbia. I am an associate justice-designate of the Supreme Court of the United States and received Senate confirmation on April 7, 2022. I am the first Black woman and the first former federal public defender to serve on the Supreme Court.

1. Which Supreme Court Justice did I clerk for?
   A. Sonia Sotomayor
   B. Clarence Thomas
   C. Stephen Breyer
2. What year did I graduate Juris Doctor cum laude?
   A. 1992
   B. 1996
   C. 1988
3. I am the first black woman to?
   A. Serve on U.S. District Court
   B. Serve on U.S. Court of Appeals
   C. Serve on U.S. Supreme Court

Directions: Find the words associated with Ketanji's life and career.

```
C J R E Y E R B N E H P E T S F T H
C O H W E C D K F N F Q V P E Z R A
L C U J T Q T A V Y P I D K J E B R
A O Y R P R F K D F I S N H C S T V
S M T Z T I U S H C A S V I Q C A A
H M T R N O E O K C E G T D P L R R
Y I S P U V F A C S N S B Q S E S D
P S P J D O A A M T U R G I A R X U
Q S L I T J C C P J C N Z R U K M N
R I V T Z S G E E P T I P P C S J I
K O R S Z X L T M C E G R X B H M V
Y N L I K P A H N E U A W T N I P E
V E I X O I P H X B R S L Y S P A R
D R S Z C U E C J Q C P I S W I Y S
M K Q O E G I X D D Q U U W Y G D I
J J S J D N Z O W P G A C S J H M T
X S Q U R X T L B Q V D V H C S E Y
A A J Q N E D I B T N E D I S E R P
```

Find These Words

COURTOFAPPEALS ASSOCIATEJUSTICE DISTRICTCOURT
HARVARDUNIVERSITY SUPREMECOURT JUDGE
CLERKSHIP STEPHENBREYER COMMISSIONER
PRESIDENTBIDEN

Directions: Read and answer the questions. These are your opinions so the answers will vary.

If you could meet a historical figure, who would it be?

What's your favorite extracurricular class?

What is your favorite thing to do over the weekends?

Directions: Read and answer the questions below. There are clues in the puzzle to help you. Try and solve the cryptic message.

Clue for cryptic message: Their movement allowed Ketanji to get this position.

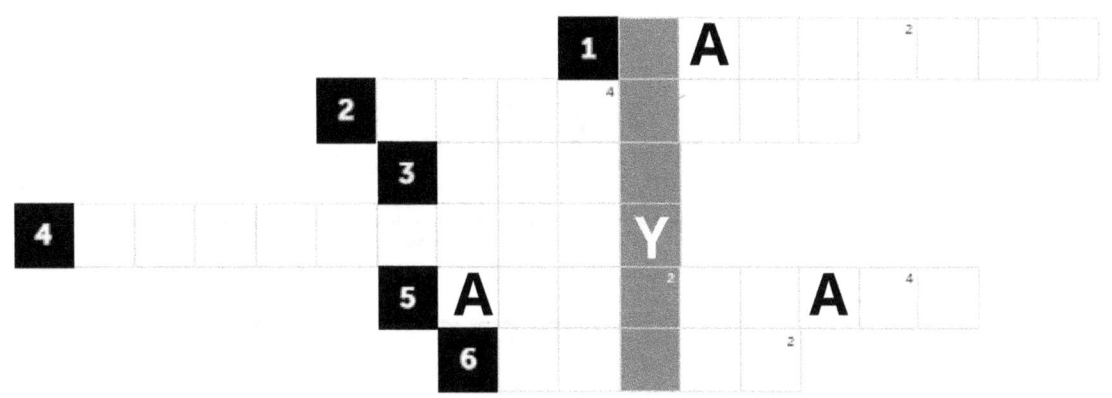

Questions

1) Ketanji graduated from Harvard with an _____ of Arts magna cum laude.

2) Ketanji was a United States circuit judge of the United States Court of Appeals for the _____ of Columbia Circuit.

3) Ketanji worked as a staff reporter and researcher at _____ Magazine.

4) Ketanji has not given any particular judicial _____ that she uses.

5) Ketanji was an _____ specialist in private practice at the law firm of Morrison & Foerster.

6) Ketanji became the first Black woman to _____ on the Supreme Court.

Directions: This is the WGLT Challenge. Solve the cryptogram. As the puzzle solver, you need to find which number belongs to which character. And this can be pretty challenging! You will need to match the number with the letter. There are some letters given to you below. This will help you solve the other words and unlock more characters. **Good Luck.**

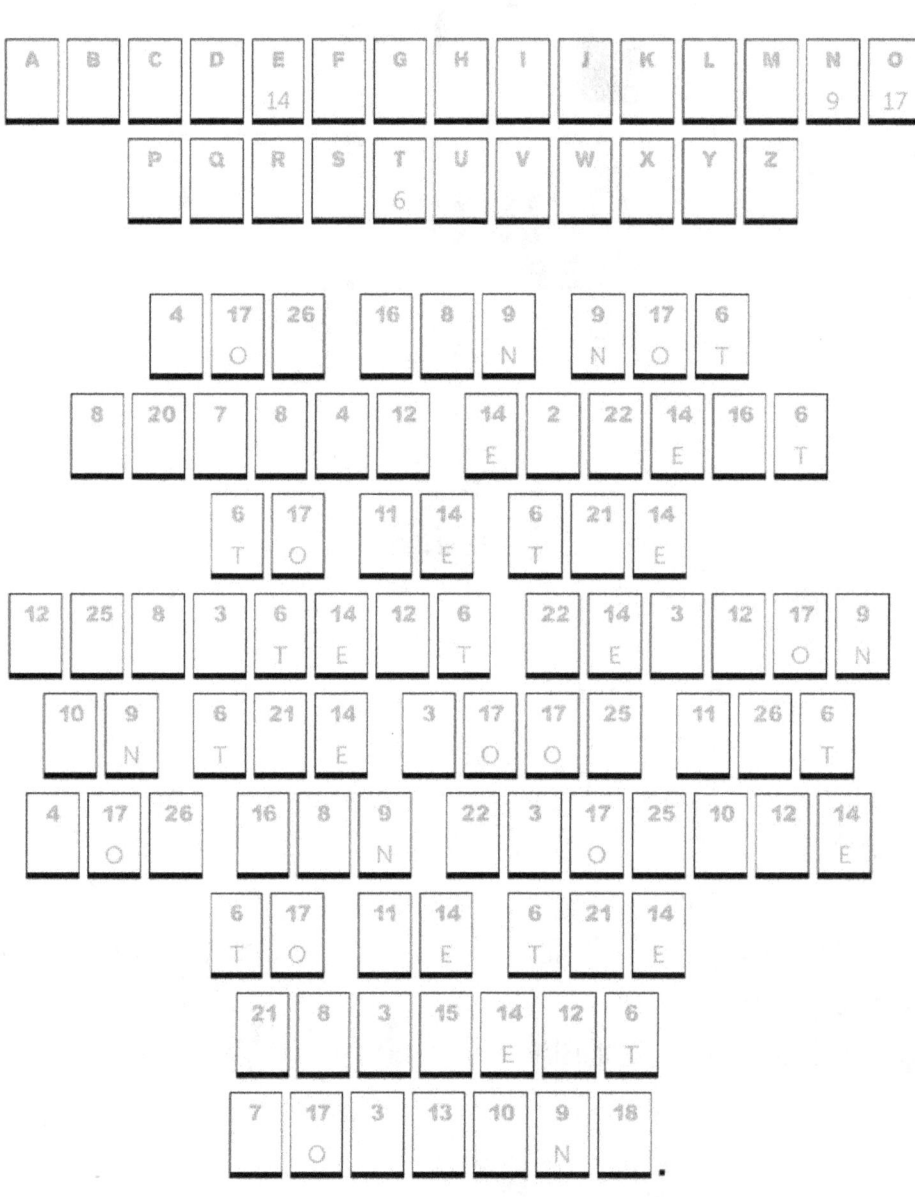

Darryl E. Evans

Darryl E. Evans

November 24, 1961 – February 26, 2014
CHEF

179

Darryl E. Evans

Darryl E. Evans

Darryl E. Evans

Darryl E. Evans

Darryl E. Evans

Darryl E. Evans

Directions: read the bio below and answer the following questions.

Hi, my name is Darryl E. Evans. I was born on November 24, 1961, in Columbus, GA. I graduated from Carver High School in 1979. I studied business administration at Chattahoochee Valley Community College in 1981. I graduated from the American Culinary Federation (AFC) apprenticeship program at Georgia State University in 1986. I became a certified working chef in 1991. I won the AFC's Chef of the Year award three times. I was the first African American to participate in the International Culinary Olympics in Frankfurt, Germany, where I won three gold medals and one silver medal in 1988 and 1992. I won numerous awards and served as a visiting chef for functions that were held by the United States Congress and various state governments. I was named Chef and Culinarian of the Year by the Greater Atlanta Chef's Association in 1991, 1993 and 1996.

1. What was the name of the college I attended?
    A. Georgia University
    B. Chattahoochee Valley Community College
    C. Georgia State University
2. What year did I become a certified Chef?
    A. 1986
    B. 1992
    C. 1991
3. I won___ gold medals at the Culinary Olympics?
    A. two
    B. one
    C. three

Directions: Answer the questions, to solve the crossword puzzle. You can use the internet if you get stuck on any question.

Across

1) Darryl became a Certified _____ in just five years.

7) Darryl was the morning sous-chef at the _____.

8) Darryl was the first African-American member of the U.S. Culinary _____ team.

Down

2) Darryl won two individuals _____ and team gold and silver medals at the Culinary Olympics.

3) One of Darryl's specialties was his _____ With Spiced Cream Cheese Icing.

4) Darryl helped open the _____ Restaurant in Atlanta.

5) Darryl was the _____ chef of the Athens, Ga., Country Club.

6) Darryl was in _____ for two years in high school.

Directions: Read and answer the questions. These are your opinions so the answers will vary.

If you could go back to any period in time, which would you choose?

What's your favorite breakfast food?

What is a unique talent you have?

Directions: Unscramble the words below about Darryl. See if you can get the bonus word.

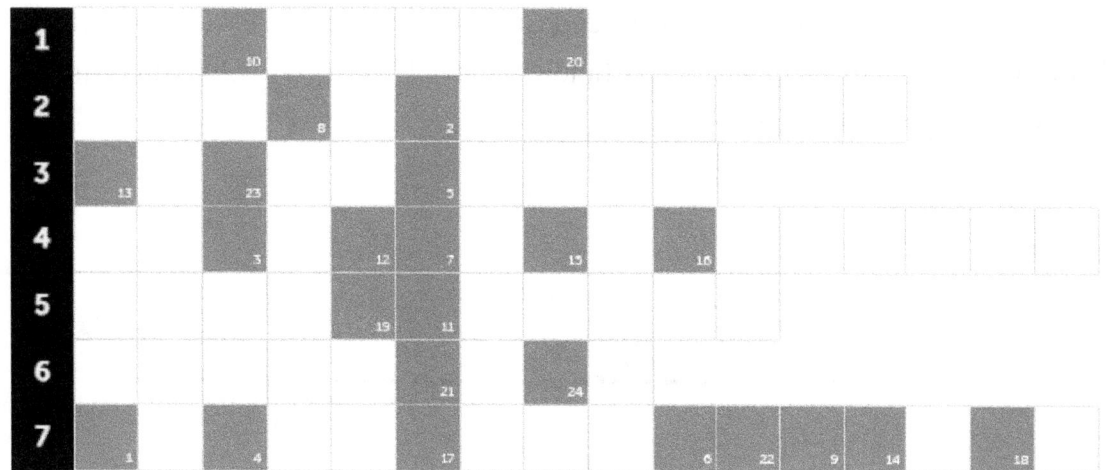

BONUS WORD

Unscramble Words

1) uusbmcol
2) ecichueetxfev
3) epaeripntc
4) mclnusyacyolprii
5) omndvfideia
6) cfeo-shsu
7) uzraaattaaselenr

185

Directions: This is the WGLT Challenge. Solve the cryptogram. As the puzzle solver, you need to find which number belongs to which character. And this can be pretty challenging! You will need to match the number with the letter. There are some letters given to you below. This will help you solve the other words and unlock more characters. **Good Luck.**

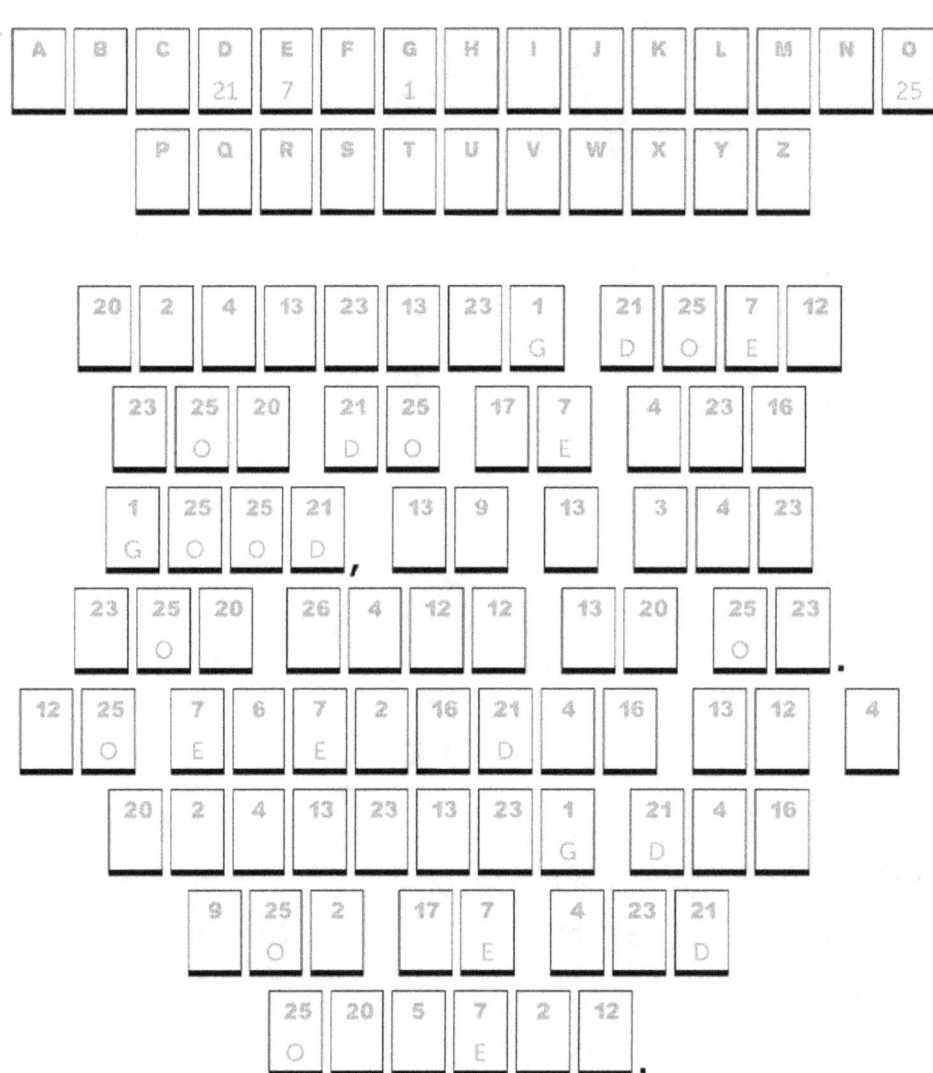

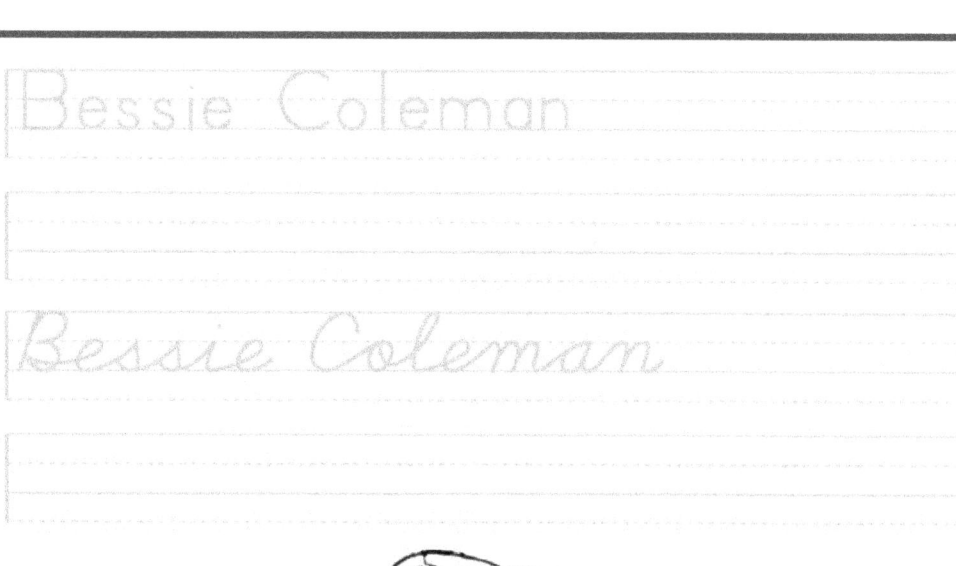

January 26, 1892 – April 30, 1926
CIVIL AVIATOR

187

LEFT BLANK ON PURPOSE

Bessie Coleman

Bessie Coleman

Bessie Coleman

Bessie Coleman

Bessie Coleman

Bessie Coleman

Directions: read the bio below and answer the following questions.

Hi, my name is Elizabeth Coleman. I was born on January 26, 1892, in Atlanta, TX. When I was young, I was given the nickname "Bessie." I attended Missionary Baptist Church School. In 1910, I attended Oklahoma Colored Agricultural and Normal University but never finished. In 1915, I moved to Chicago, IL. After hearing my brothers' stories of female pilots in France, I wanted to become a pilot. I ended up going to France in 1920 because no school would take me in the U.S. I learned to fly in a Nieuport 564 biplane. In 1921, I became the first Black woman and first Native American to earn an aviation pilot's license and the first Black person and first Native American to earn an international aviation license from the Fédération Aéronautique Internationale. I became a "barnstorming" stunt flier. I became known as "Queen Bess" and performed in many stunt airshows, including in 1922 at an event that honored the veterans of the all-Black 369th Infantry Regiment of World War I.

1. What was my nickname for me?
    A. Lizzy
    B. Bessie
    C. Beth
2. I'm the first black woman to?
    A. earn an aviation pilot's license
    B. earn a Truck Driving license
    C. earn an Engineer's license
3. What type of pilot was I?
    A. Commercial
    B. Stunt
    C. War

Directions: Find the words associated with Bessie's life and career.

U	S	P	D	V	F	T	S	I	R	U	C	I	N	A	M	R	B
R	I	M	I	N	R	Q	Z	V	H	N	M	T	A	V	R	J	K
U	S	G	J	L	K	L	G	I	J	U	R	V	B	E	S	N	W
S	O	M	S	V	O	E	T	E	D	F	I	V	K	R	Q	E	K
F	O	T	S	Q	G	T	H	R	J	A	H	K	E	F	G	N	K
Z	N	E	E	W	X	M	L	R	T	I	W	I	R	A	M	P	N
M	A	X	B	O	B	F	S	I	O	U	L	L	U	D	A	T	V
U	P	A	-	P	F	K	O	K	C	F	X	G	O	R	X	Y	O
N	U	S	N	D	H	N	Z	A	-	E	N	T	I	C	G	N	P
F	J	F	E	T	Z	Q	K	T	O	A	N	S	R	J	V	N	I
L	X	M	E	X	S	U	N	N	L	W	X	S	Y	N	A	E	K
E	N	L	U	D	Y	U	O	-	V	E	F	L	E	O	V	J	Z
X	S	V	Q	D	T	Q	H	G	S	F	F	Y	F	S	V	V	C
Y	Y	D	Q	S	U	C	D	B	A	Z	K	I	A	X	X	J	I
L	W	M	M	B	N	J	C	L	U	C	E	J	J	U	B	G	E
K	P	K	Y	E	X	K	D	C	Z	R	I	M	S	E	I	Z	H
G	N	U	R	J	D	M	G	L	P	M	L	H	G	G	J	P	R
F	R	F	Y	J	P	O	F	V	E	V	X	F	C	N	Q	M	O

Find These Words

CHICAGO AVIATION JENNY
TEXAS PILOTLICENSE MANICURIST
FRENCH-LANGUAGE PARIS STUNT-FLIER
QUEEN-BESS

Directions: Read and answer the questions. These are your opinions so the answers will vary.

If you could meet a cartoon character in real life, who would you pick?

Who is a friend at school that you know you can count on?

What is one thing you want to know about your teacher?

Directions: Read and answer the questions below. There are clues in the puzzle to help you. Try and solve the cryptic message.

Clue for cryptic message: Bessie love to do these.

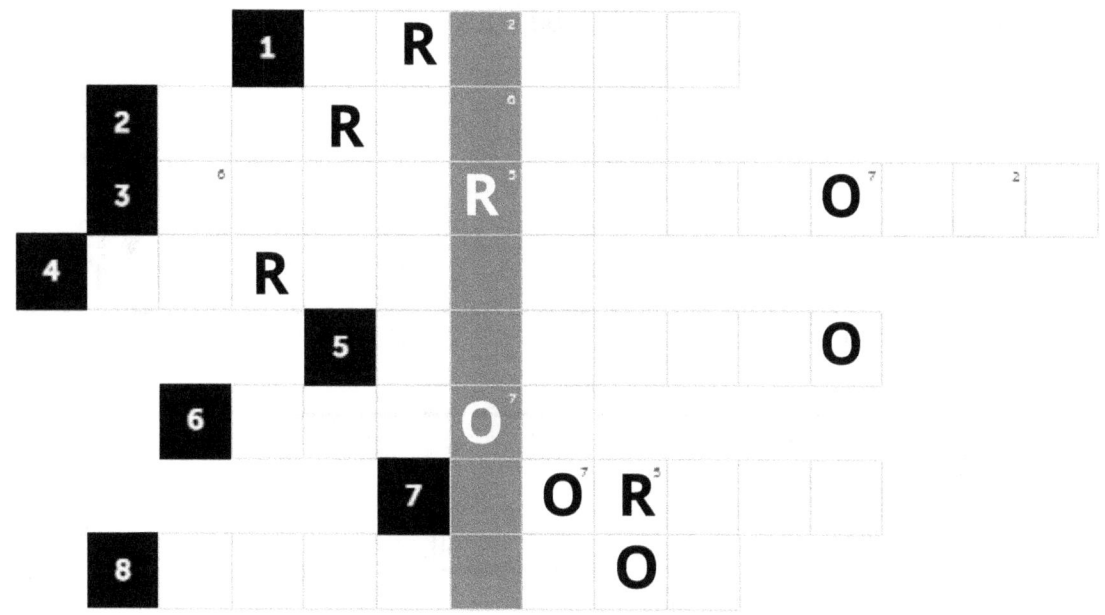

Questions

1) Bessie relocated to _____ where she enrolled in Caudron Brothers School of Aviation where she specialized in stunt flying and parachuting.

2) Bessie learned to speak French at the _____ school in the Chicago Loop.

3) Bessie was the first black person and first Native American to earn an _____ aviation license from the Fédération Aéronautique Internationale.

4) Bessie purchased a _____ JN-4 (Jenny), which was unfortunately the same plane she died in due to a wrench jamming the controls.

5) April 29th is Bessie Coleman Day in _____, the city that inspired her career.

6) In 1921, Bessie became the first black woman and first Native American to earn an aviation _____ license

7) Bessie _____ as a manicurist before she went to flying school.

8) Bessie attended _____ University in Oklahoma where her dad stayed.

Directions: This is the WGLT Challenge. Solve the cryptogram. As the puzzle solver, you need to find which number belongs to which character. And this can be pretty challenging! You will need to match the number with the letter. There are some letters given to you below. This will help you solve the other words and unlock more characters. **Good Luck.**

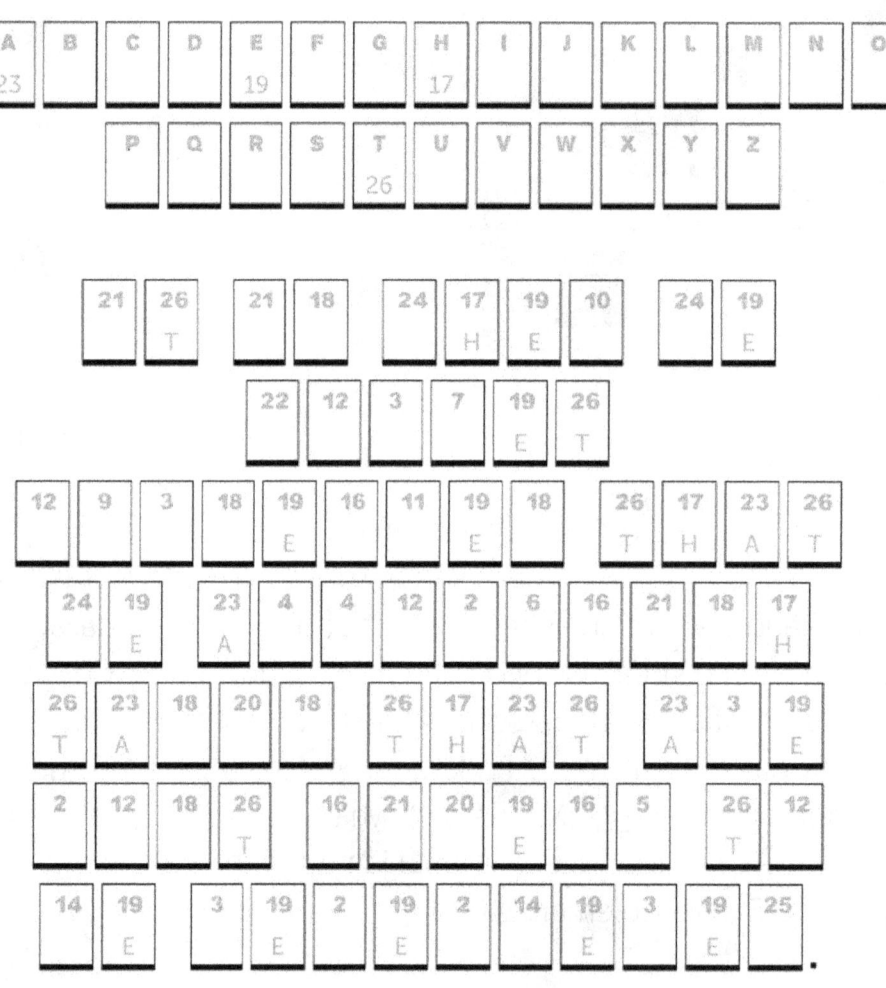

John W Cromwell Jr

John W Cromwell Jr

August 2, 1883 – December 16, 1971
CERTIFIED PUBLIC ACCOUNTANTS(CPA)

LEFT BLANK ON PURPOSE

John W Cromwell Jr.

John W Cromwell Jr.

John W Cromwell Jr.

John W Cromwell Jr.

John W Cromwell Jr.

John W Cromwell Jr.

Directions: read the bio below and answer the following questions.

Hi, my name is John Wesley Cromwell Jr. I was born on August 2, 1883, in Dorchester County, MD. I graduated from Dartmouth in 1906 and in 1907, I earned a master's degree from Dartmouth. I also became a member of Phi Beta Kappa. I taught mathematics at Paul Laurence Dunbar High School, which was a prestigious Black high school. I wanted to become a certified public accountant (CPA), but it wasn't easy since I was not allowed to sit for the CPA exam in Washington, D.C., Virginia, or Maryland. African Americans could not get a CPA license due to the experience requirement. New Hampshire passed a law that allowed people to obtain a CPA license without the experience requirement. Thanks to that change, I passed the CPA exam and was initially licensed in 1921 in New Hampshire. After I was certified, I continued to teach high school accounting but also opened my own CPA firm in the Washington, D.C. area. I was the nation's first Black CPA.

1. What college do I graduate from?
    A. Dartmouth College
    B. Colby-Sawyer College
    C. Keene State College
2. What year did I become a CPA?
    A. 1907
    B. 1923
    C. 1921
3. What did I teach when I first started teaching?
    A. English
    B. Mathematics
    C. History

Directions: Answer the questions, to solve the crossword puzzle. You can use the internet if you get stuck on any question.

Across

1) John was the first Black accountant inducted into the Accounting _____.

3) John served as _____ of Howard University.

5) John became a licensed Certified Public Accountant in 1921 in _____.

6) John _____ in his own CPA firm in the Washington DC area.

7) John was a member of Phi Beta Kappa, a _____ academic honor society.

8) John taught high school _____ because of limited practice opportunities.

Down

2) John was the first Black Certified Public _____.

4) John graduated with honors from _____ College.

Directions: Read and answer the questions. These are your opinions so the answers will vary.

If you could meet one celebrity, who would it be?

What is something that you are thankful for?

What is a family tradition that you have?

Directions: Unscramble the words below about John. See if you can get the bonus word.

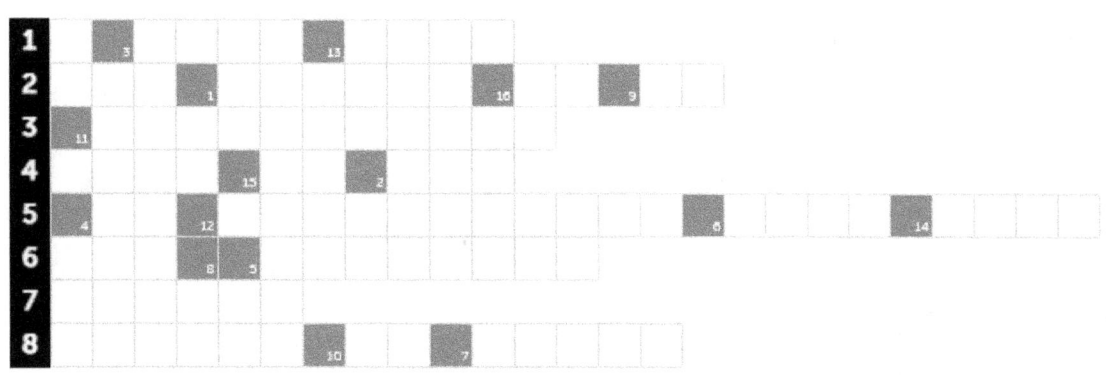

BONUS WORD

| 6 | 7 | 8 | 9 | 10 | 11 | 12 | 13 | 14 | 15 | 16 |

Unscramble Words

1) ttciemshama **2)** hohhocudinasrlbg **3)** sprnwihhmeea
4) crlmrlpoote **5)** iinnlercpeibuuaoctttfcacd **6)** rckdabylaobaw
7) owhadr **8)** umlcretogldhaot

201

Directions: This is the WGLT Challenge. Solve the cryptogram. As the puzzle solver, you need to find which number belongs to which character. And this can be pretty challenging! You will need to match the number with the letter. There are some letters given to you below. This will help you solve the other words and unlock more characters. **Good Luck.**

Booker Washington Answers

1. **What did I found in 1900?**
   A. NAACP
   B. NNBL
   C. CORE
2. **I became President of Tuskegee University in?**
   A. 1881
   B. 1890
   C. 1900
3. **I was the first African American in the U.S. to what?**
   A. Be Freed
   B. Be a millionaire
   C. Be on a U.S. postage stamp

Crossword 1

Across:
2. CARNEGIE HALL
4. SCHOOL
7. EMANCIPATION
8. MARK TWAIN

Down:
1. FINANCIAL
3. FUNDRAISERS
6. TFT

Crossword 2

1. ORATOR
2. ADVISER
3. EDUCATOR
4. TUSKEGEE INSTITUTE
5. REPUBLICAN
6. HAMPTON INSTITUTE
7. PRESIDENT ROOSEVELT
8. ATLANTA COMPROMISE
9. AGRICULTURAL INSTITUTE
10. SLAVERY

NATIONAL NEGRO BUSINESS LEAGUE

Cipher Key

A	B	C	D	E	F	G	H	I	J	K	L	M	N	O	P	Q	R	S	T	U	V
2	3	25	11	23	10	26	21	14	22	19	6	12	7	1	9	8	24	5	17	16	18

W	X	Y	Z
15	4	13	20

"ASSOCIATE YOURSELF WITH PEOPLE OF GOOD QUALITY, FOR IT IS BETTER TO BE ALONE THAN IN BAD COMPANY."

1. What college did I graduate from?
   A. Howard University
   B. Alabama State University
   C. Jackson State University
2. What sorority did I found in 1908?
   A. Delta Sigma Theta
   B. Alpha Kappa Alpha
   C. Zeta Phi Beta
3. What was my Bachelors Degree in?
   A. Science
   B. Mathematics
   C. Liberal Arts

Ethel Hedgemon
Answers

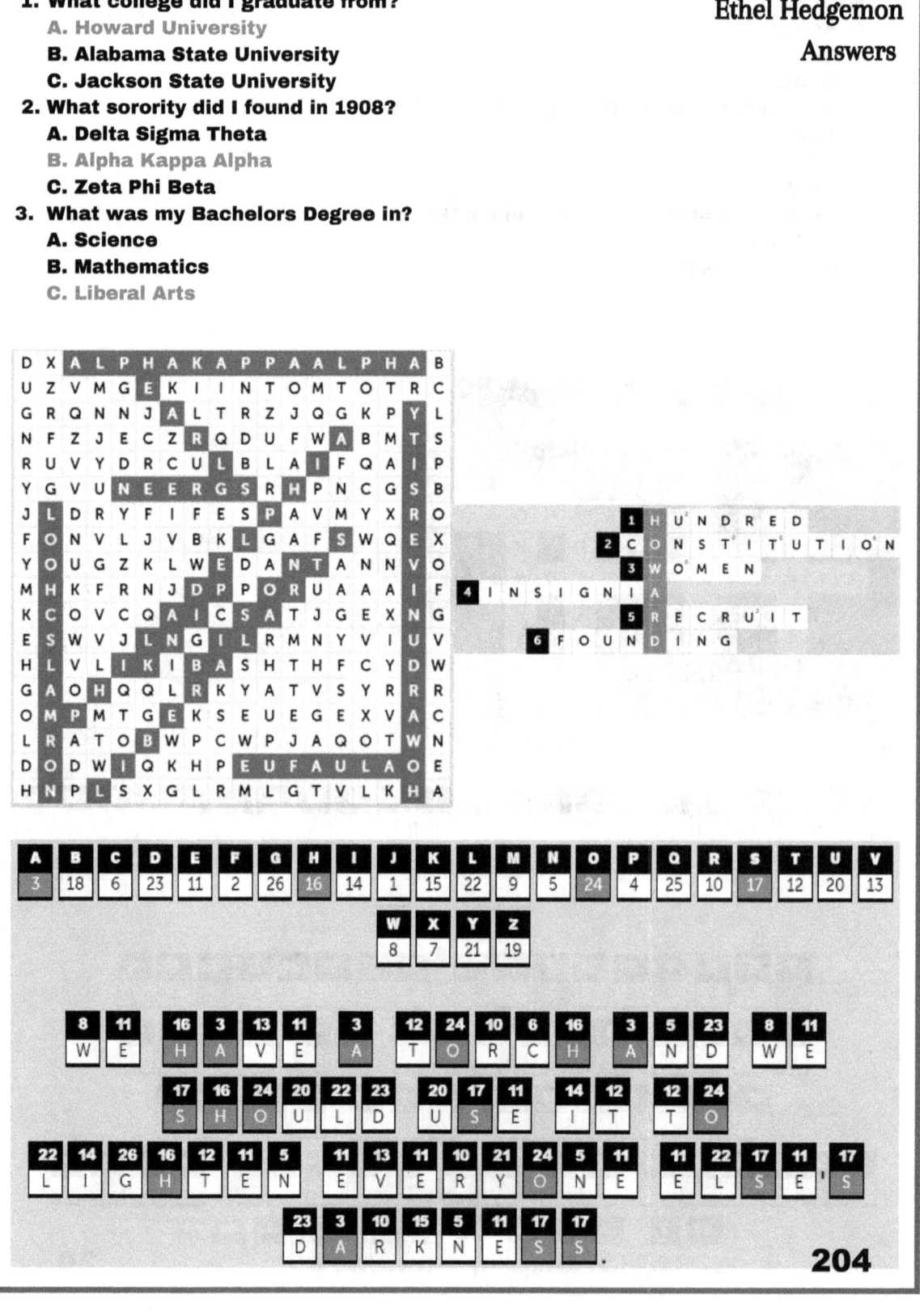

"WE HAVE A TORCH AND WE SHOULD USE IT TO LIGHTEN EVERYONE ELSE'S DARKNESS."

204

1. What was the name of the test I created for syphilis?
   A. Syphilis test
   B. Hinton test
   C. Chemiluminescence immunoassays test
2. What college did I graduate from?
   A. Yale
   B. Harvard
   C. Princeton
3. I was the first Black scientist to become a member of?
   A. National Honor Society
   B. American Society of Addiction Medicine
   C. American Society for Microbiology

William Hinton
Answers

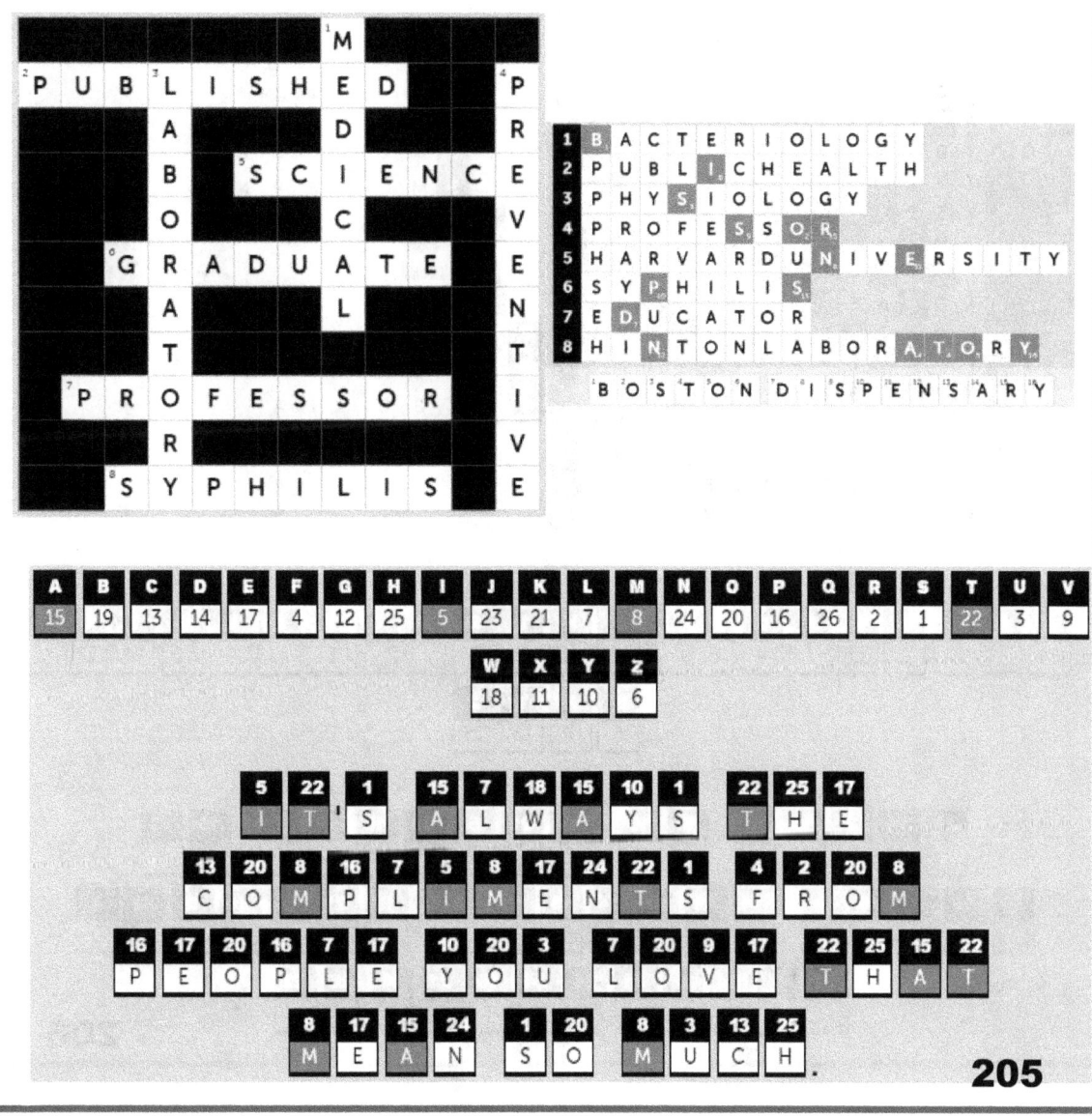

Mae Jemison Answers

1. What college did I get my medical degree from?
   A. Cornell University
   B. Stanford University
   C. Harvard University
2. How old was I when I started college?
   A. 18
   B. 16
   C. 19
3. I was the first African American woman to what?
   A. Fly a plane
   B. Travel into space
   C. Teach at Cornell University

Crossword:
1. CHEMICAL
2. DANCER
3. MODERN
4. INTERNATIONAL
5. EARTH
6. UNIVERSITY
7. NATIONAL
8. FREQUENCIES
9. LIBERIA

A	B	C	D	E	F	G	H	I	J	K	L	M	N	O	P	Q	R	S	T	U	V
24	18	20	1	19	3	4	8	21	12	11	15	5	26	10	14	23	9	22	16	17	2

W	X	Y	Z
6	7	13	25

"NEVER BE LIMITED BY OTHER PEOPLE'S LIMITED IMAGINATIONS."

206

James McCune Smith
Answers

1. **What is my highest level of education?**
   A. Ph. D
   B. Masters Degree
   C. Bachelors Degree
2. **I was the first African American in U.S. to what?**
   A. To travel to a different country
   B. To go to college overseas
   C. To run a pharmacy
3. **Where did I go to college at?**
   A. United States
   B. Scotland
   C. England

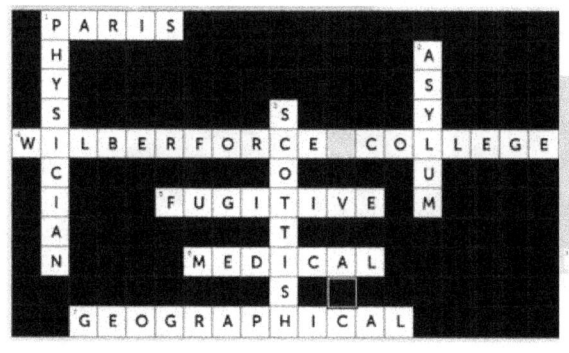

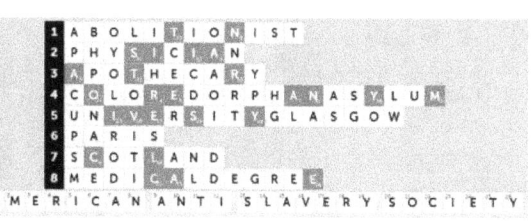

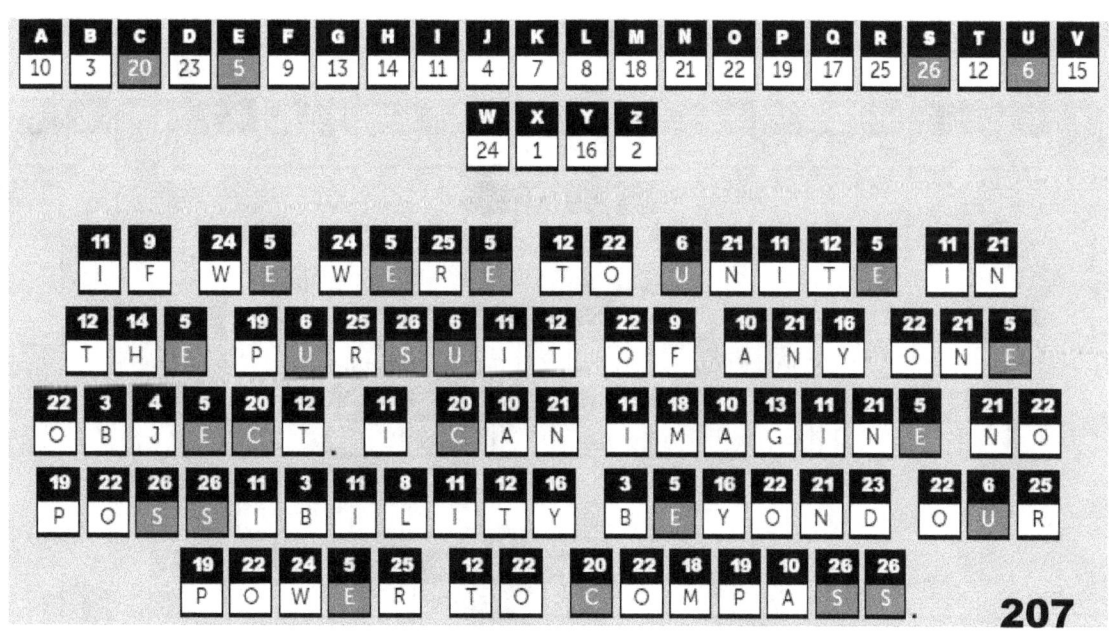

"IF WE WERE TO UNITE IN THE PURSUIT OF ANY ONE OBJECT, I CAN IMAGINE NO POSSIBILITY BEYOND OUR POWER TO COMPASS."

207

1. In 1879 I graduated and became a what?
   A. Doctor
   B. Nurse
   C. Nurses Aid
2. What year did I help found NACGN?
   A. 1896
   B. 1908
   C. 1900
3. How long was the program to become a nurse?
   A. 12 months
   B. 6 months
   C. 16 months

Mary Eliza Mahoney
Answers

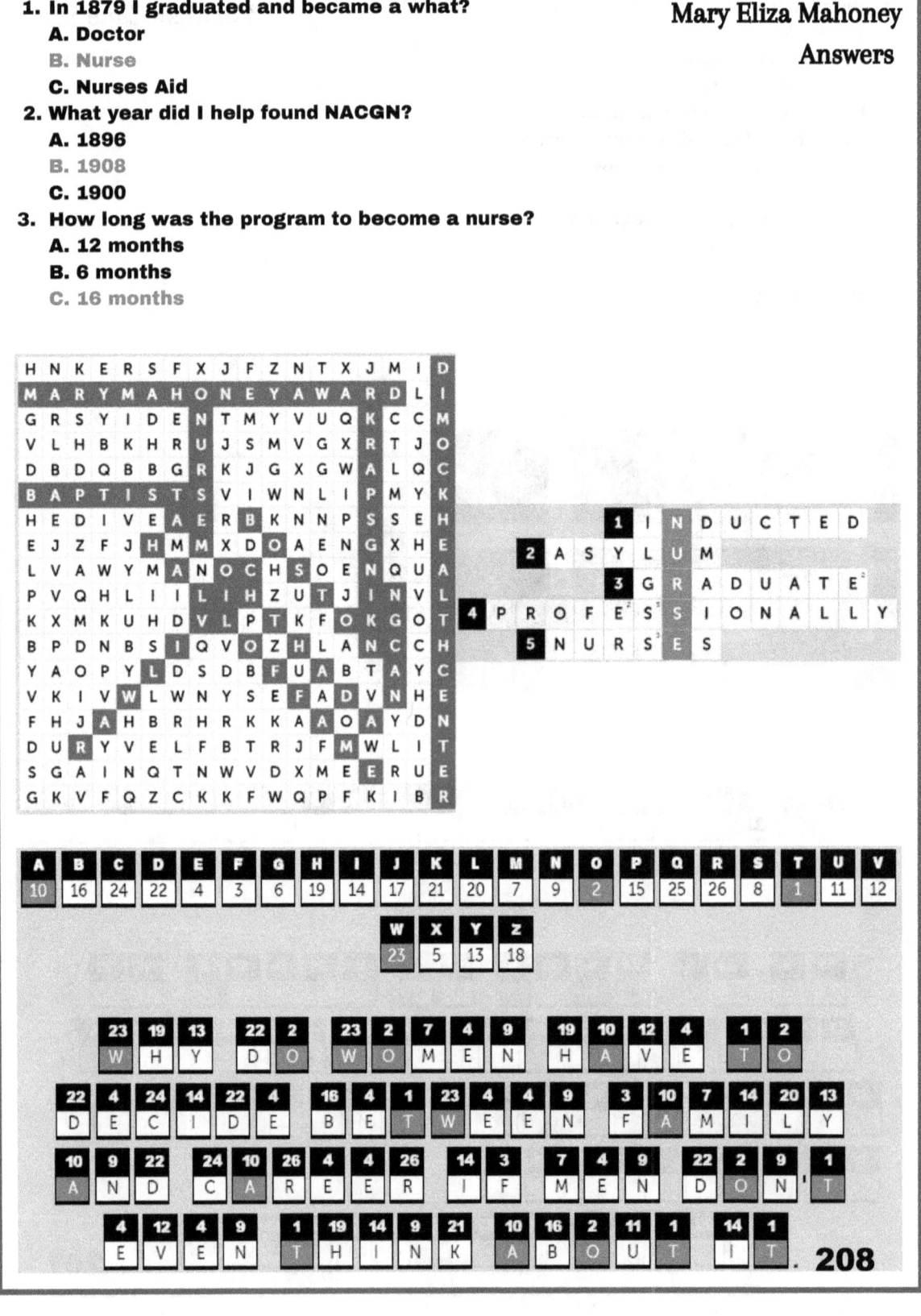

"WHY DO WOMEN HAVE TO DECIDE BETWEEN FAMILY AND CAREER IF MEN DON'T EVEN THINK ABOUT IT."

208

1. What State did I help survey?
   A. Virginia
   B. Delaware
   C. Washington D.C.
2. What did I successfully predict?
   A. The next President
   B. A Solar Eclipse
   C. The freeing of slaves
3. I primarily worked where?
   A. At the Capitol
   B. The farm
   C. With Major Ellicott

Benjamin Banneker
Answers

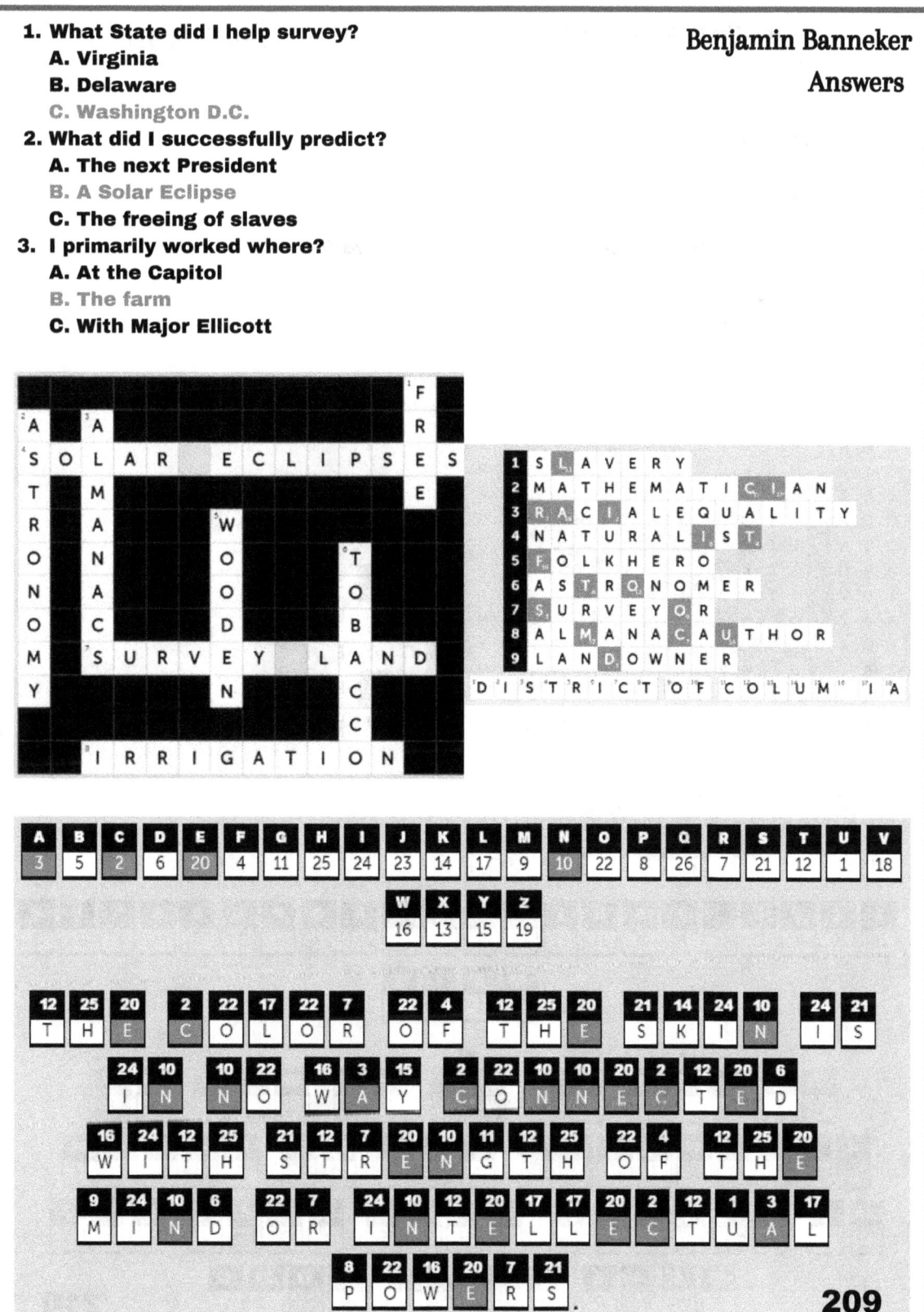

"THE COLOR OF THE SKIN IS IN NO WAY CONNECTED WITH STRENGTH OF THE MIND OR INTELLECTUAL POWERS."

Fanny Jackson Coppin
Answers

1. I wasn't the first African American woman to what?
   A. Principal
   B. Superintendent
   C. Student
2. What year did I graduate from college?
   A. 1860
   B. 1863
   C. 1865
3. I was the first African American to do what at Oberlin?
   A. Graduate
   B. Teacher
   C. Valedictorian

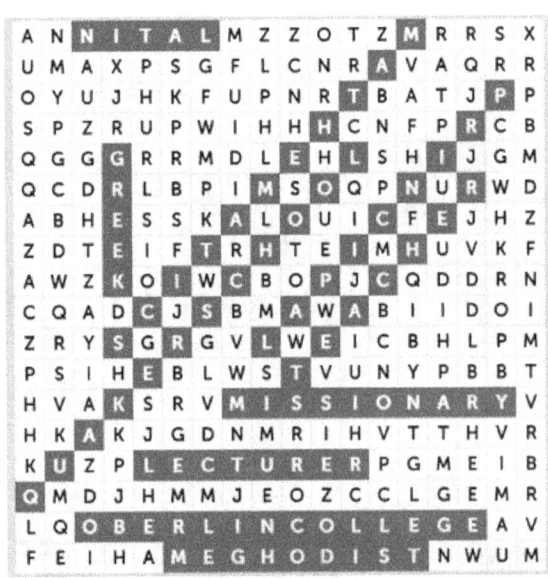

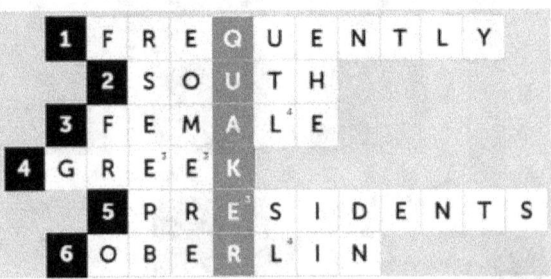

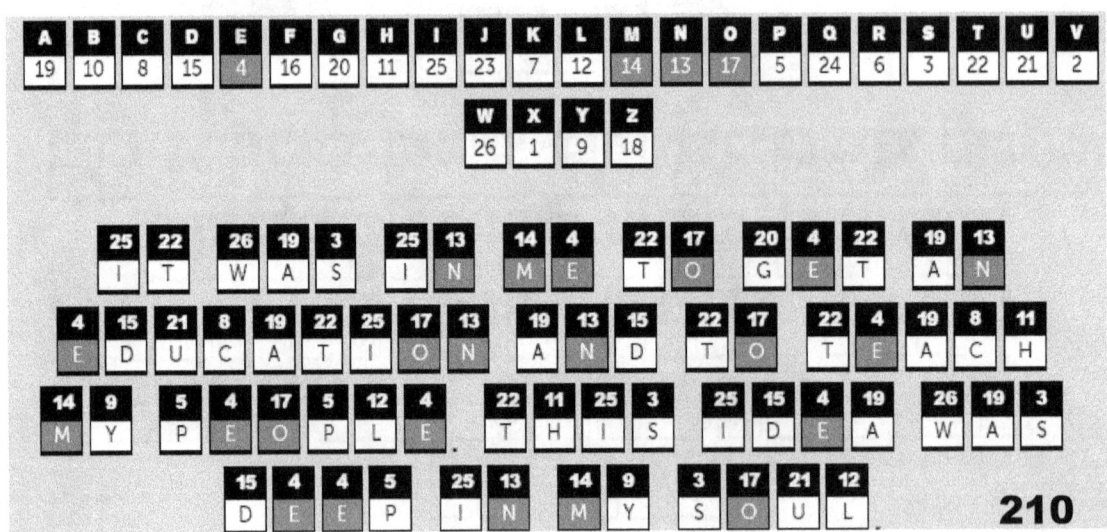

IT WAS IN ME TO GET AN EDUCATION AND TO TEACH MY PEOPLE. THIS IDEA WAS DEEP IN MY SOUL

210

1. **What film did I act, write and produce?**
   A. Guava Island
   B. Magic Mike XXL
   C. The To Do List
2. **What college did I go to?**
   A. UCLA
   B. University of Georgia
   C. New York University
3. **What award did I win for writing on 30 Rock?**
   A. Image Award
   B. Emmys
   C. Writers Guild of America Award

Donald Glover
Answers

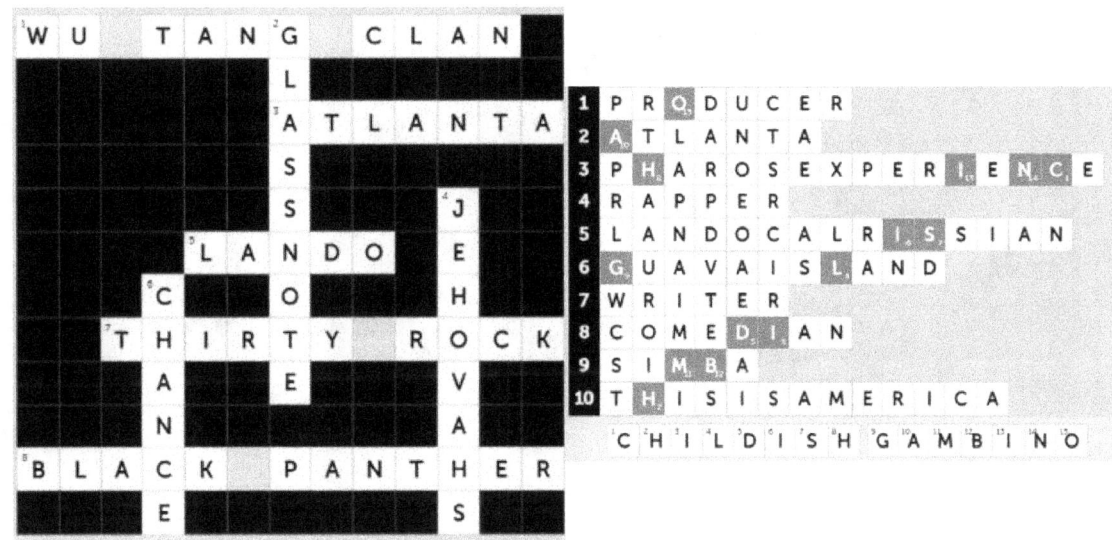

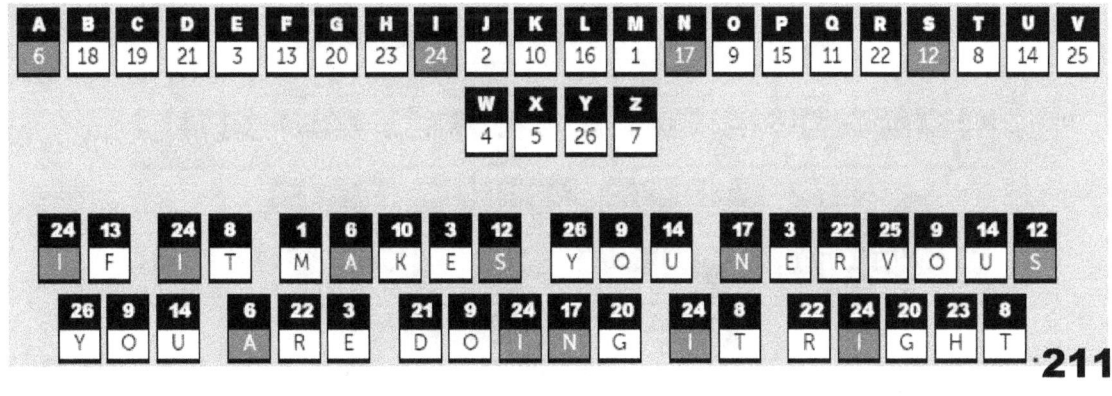

IF IT MAKES YOU NERVOUS
YOU ARE DOING IT RIGHT

Robin Roberts Answers

1. **What was my first broadcasting job for?**
   A. WLOX-TV
   B. WSMV-TV
   C. WDAM-TV

2. **What year did I start working for GMA?**
   A. 1995
   B. 2005
   C. 1990

3. **What college did I graduate from?**
   A. Southeastern Louisiana University
   B. Louisiana State University
   C. Tuskegee University

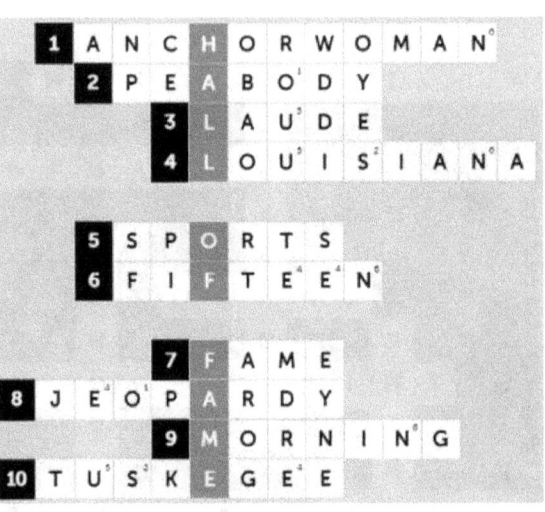

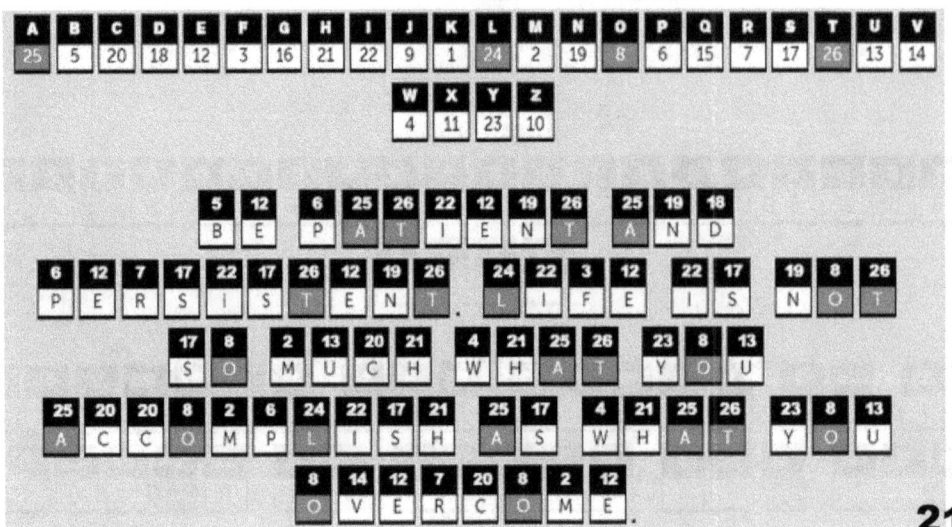

"Be patient and persistent. Life is not so much what you accomplish as what you overcome."

212

William Edward Burghardt Du Bois

Answers

1. I was the first African American to do what at Harvard?
   A. Get a Bachelors degree
   B. Get a Ph. D
   C. Get a Maters degree
2. What year did I co-found NACCP?
   A. 1900
   B. 1899
   C. 1909
3. What college did I get my Bachelors Degree from?
   A. University of Berlin
   B. Fisk University
   C. Harvard University

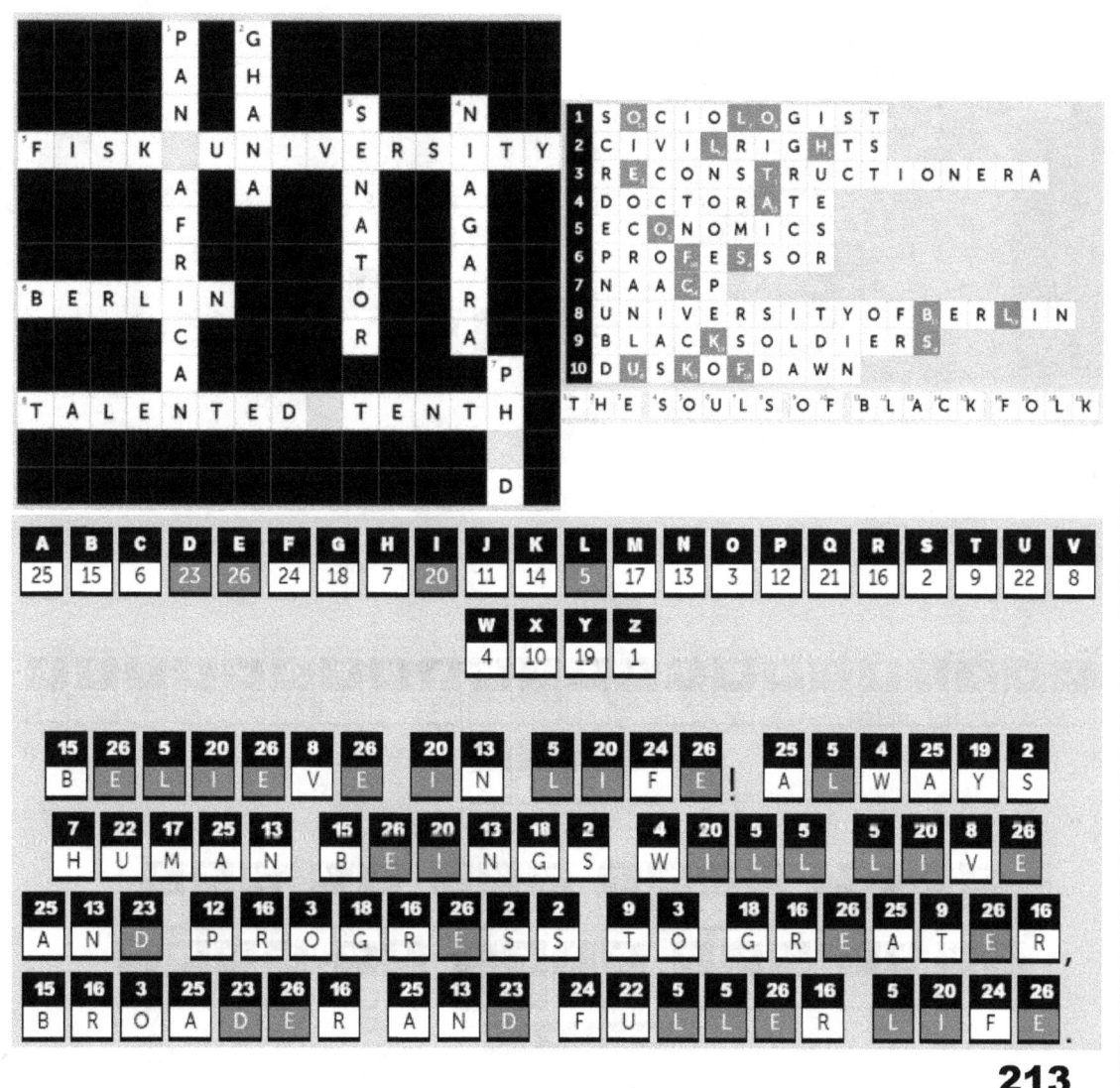

213

1. How old was I when I graduated college?
   A. 14
   B. 18
   C. 22
2. What year did I start working for NASA?
   A. 1953
   B. 1961
   C. 1958
3. What is the name of my sorority?
   A. Sigma Gamma Rho
   B. Zeta Phi Beta
   C. Alpha Kappa Alpha

Creola Katherine Coleman

Answers

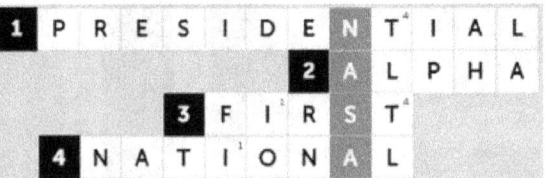

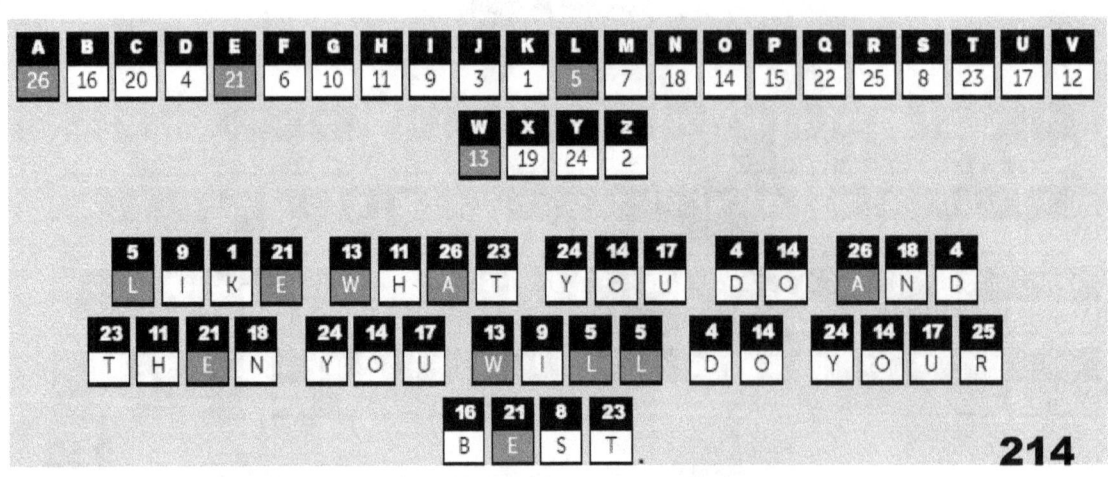

LIKE WHAT YOU DO AND THEN YOU WILL DO YOUR BEST.

214

Carter G. Woodson
Answers

1. What was my Bachelors Degree in?
   A. History
   B. Science
   C. Literature
2. I wasn't a member of what fraternity?
   A. Sigma Pi Phi
   B. Alpha Phi Alpha
   C. Omega Psi Phi
3. What did I found in 1915?
   A. NAACP
   B. UNIA
   C. ASLNH

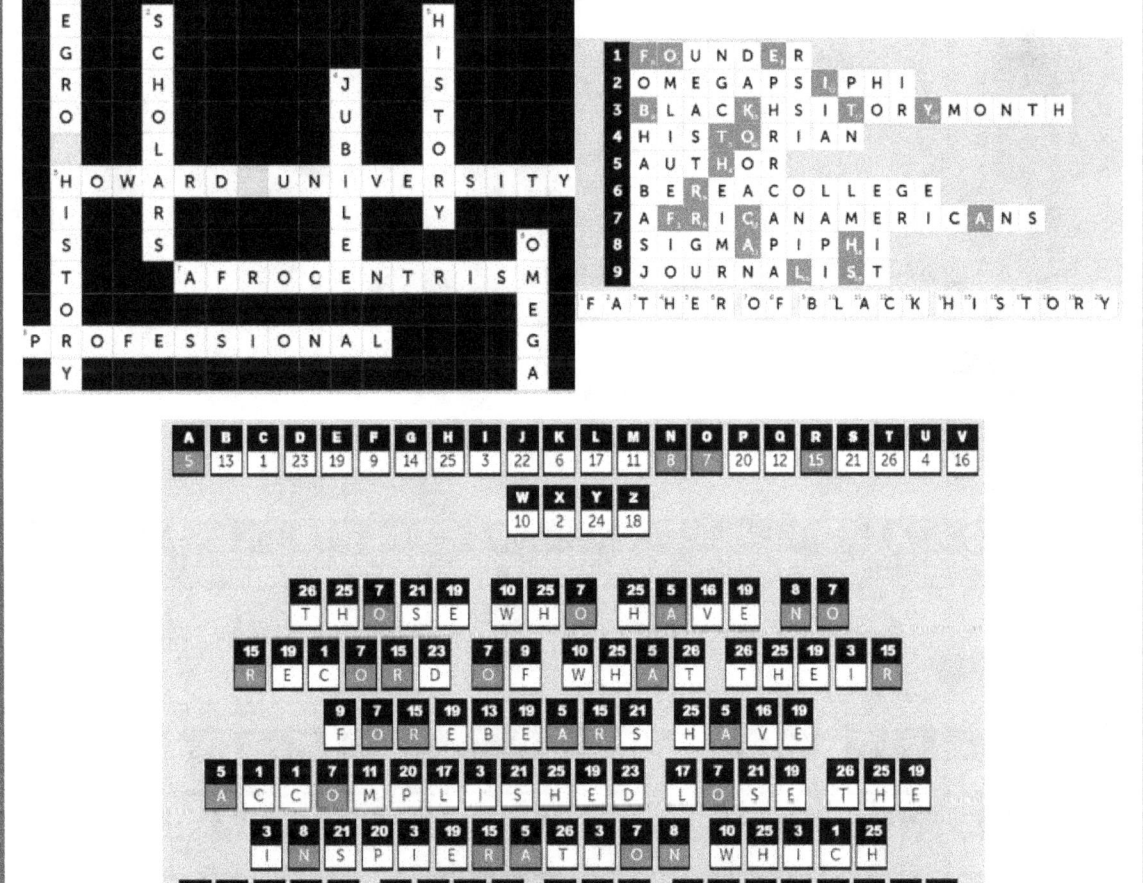

"Those who have no record of what their forebears have accomplished lose the inspieration which comes from the teaching of biography and history."

215

Shonda Rhimes Answers

1. What college did I get my Masters from?
   A. Dartmouth
   B. University of Chicago
   C. USC
2. What year did Scandal air?
   A. 2012
   B. 2018
   C. 2005
3. What did me and Debra Martin Chase work on?
   A. The Princess Diaries 2
   B. Grey's Anatomy
   C. The Princess Diaries

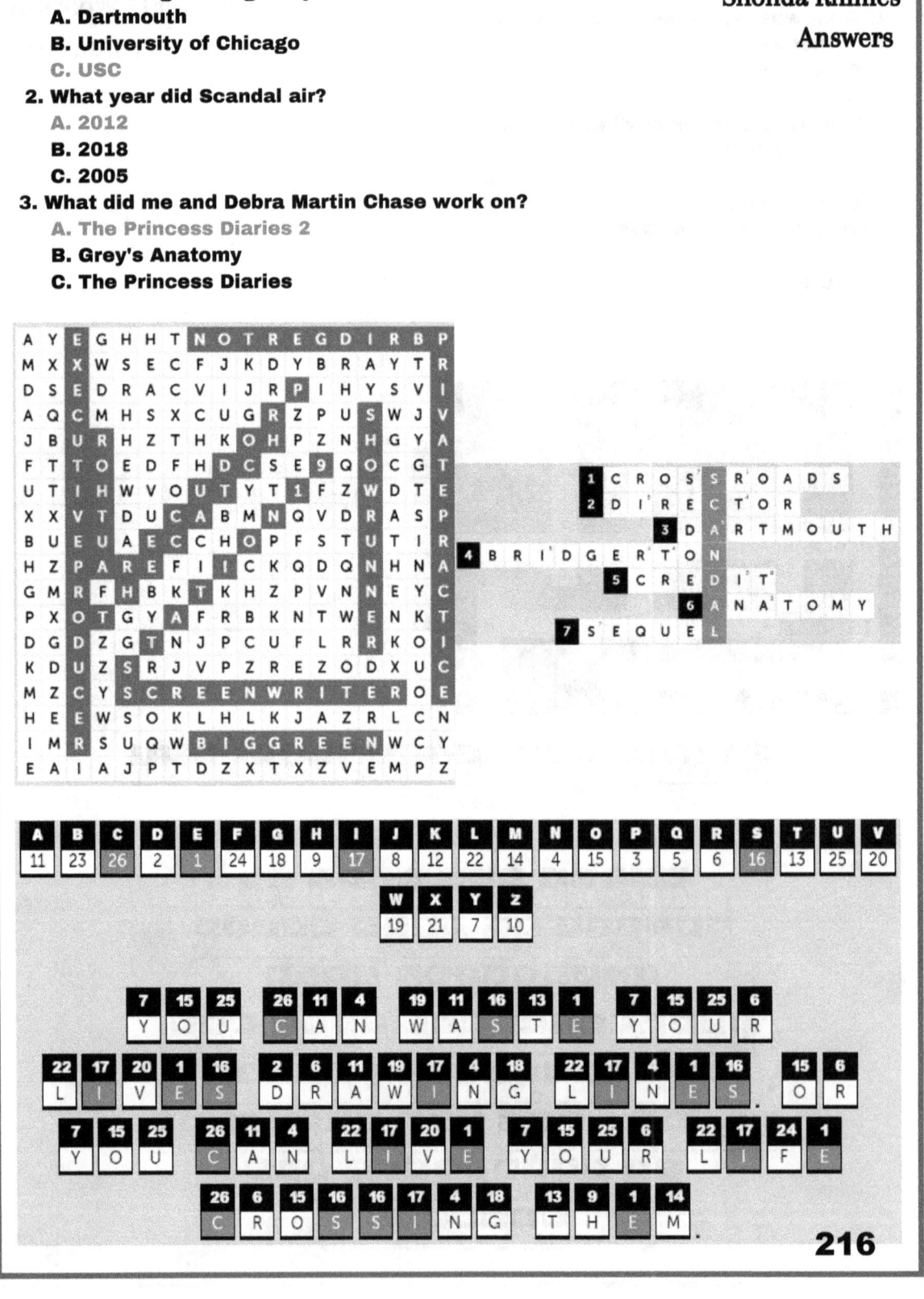

"YOU CAN WASTE YOUR LIVES DRAWING LINES. OR YOU CAN LIVE YOUR LIFE CROSSING THEM."

216

1. What was the name of the college I went to?
   A. University of Chicago
   B. Illinois University
   C. Northwestern University
2. What year did I start working for ESPN?
   A. 2005
   B. 2010
   C. 2011
3. How many Olympic games have I covered?
   A. 12
   B. 9
   C. 10

Michael Wilbon

Answers

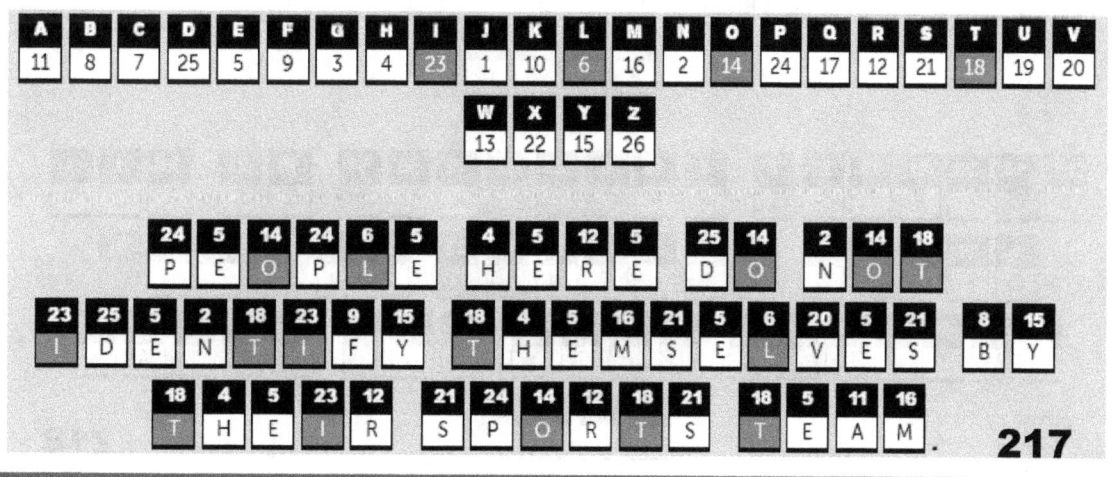

217

Rebecca Davis
Answers

1. What college did I graduate from?
   A. **New England Female Medical College**
   B. Chicago Medical College
   C. Northwestern University School of Medicine
2. What was the name of my book?
   A. Medical Mysteries
   B. Medicine from a Doctor point of view
   C. **Book of Medical Discourses**
3. I was the first African American woman in the U.S. to?
   A. Become a Nurse
   B. **Become a Doctor**
   C. Become a Teacher

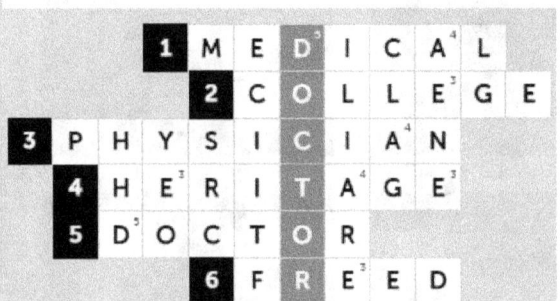

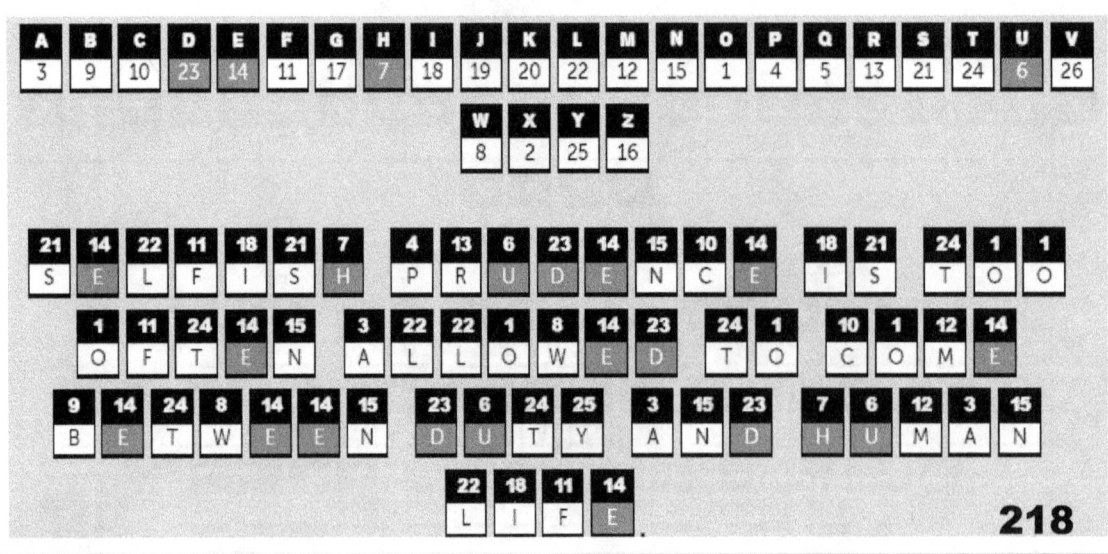

"Selfish prudence is too often allowed to come between duty and human life."

218

Stephen A Smith Answers

1. **What is my Bachelors Degree in?**
   A. Sports Medicine
   B. Mass Communication
   C. Journalism
2. **What HBCU did I graduate from?**
   A. Winston-Salem State University
   B. Fisk University
   C. Howard University
3. **What fraternity am I a member of?**
   A. Alpha Phi Alpha
   B. Kappa Alpha Psi
   C. Omega Psi Phi

Crossword Answers

Across/Down:
- P
- SOAP
- NEW YORK
- RED
- PHILADELPHIA
- FACE
- OMEGA
- QUITE
- UP
- TED
- TECHNOLOGY
- R
- BASKETBALL

1. TV PERSONALITY
2. FIRST TAKE
3. ESPN
4. COMMENTATOR
5. PHILADELPHIA INQUIRER
6. WINSTON-SALEM
7. GREENSBORO
8. BASKETBALL

THAT IS BLASPHEMOUS

Cipher Key

A	B	C	D	E	F	G	H	I	J	K	L	M	N	O	P	Q	R	S	T	U	V
24	10	18	4	23	11	9	14	20	22	17	19	21	13	12	1	15	2	7	25	16	26

W	X	Y	Z
5	3	6	8

YOU DO NOT HAVE THE RIGHT TO HOLD SOMEBODY ACCOUNTABLE FOR STANDARDS YOU REFUSE TO APPLY TO YOURSELF.

Ida Bell Wells
Answers

1. What was the city I work for in 1883?
   A. Tennessee
   B. Memphis
   C. Holly Springs
2. What year did I become editor of The Free Sprech?
   A. 1889
   B. 1892
   C. 1890
3. What was my pen name?
   A. Lizzie
   B. Bella
   C. Lola

Crossword:
1. SIBLINGS
2. WAY
3. DISCRIMINATION
4. OSCAR
5. TEACHING
6. EMANCIPATION
7. FOUNDERS
8. SUFFRAGE

A	B	C	D	E	F	G	H	I	J	K	L	M	N	O	P	Q	R	S	T	U	V
4	15	2	5	8	13	1	10	11	14	17	23	6	3	19	7	25	21	16	20	12	22

W	X	Y	Z
26	24	9	18

THE WAY TO RIGHT WRONGS IS TO TURN THE LIGHT OF TRUTH UPON THEM.

220

Mary Jane McLeod
Answers

1. What was the name of the school I started?
   A. Bethune-Cookman College
   B. Educational and Industrial Training School
   C. Cookman College
2. Bethune-Cookman College achieve full college status in?
   A. 1931
   B. 1904
   C. 1941
3. What state is Bethune-Cookman College in?
   A. South Carolina
   B. North Carolina
   C. Florida

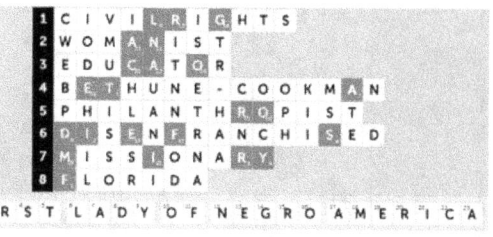

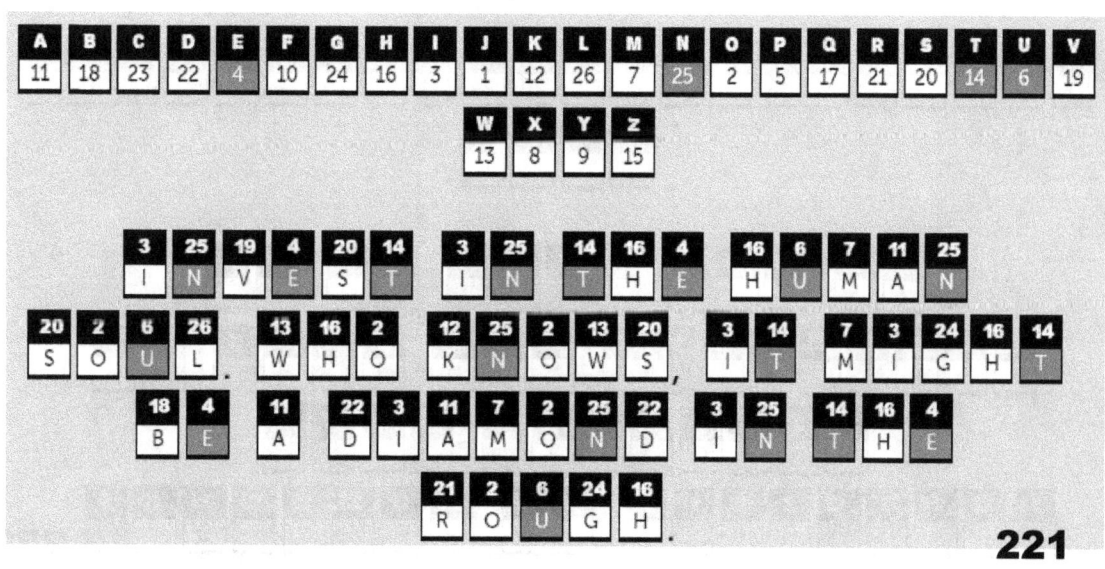

"INVEST IN THE HUMAN SOUL. WHO KNOWS, IT MIGHT BE A DIAMOND IN THE ROUGH."

221

Alexa Canady

Answers

1. What sorority am I a member of?
   A. Alpha Kappa Alpha
   B. Zeta Phi Beta
   C. Delta Sigma Theta
2. What college did I get my B.S. degree from?
   A. University of Michigan State
   B. University of Michigan
   C. University of Minnesota
3. I was the first African-American woman to be?
   A. Board-certified Neurosurgeon
   B. Board-certified Doctor
   C. Board-certified Physician

Crossword answers:
1. ZOOLOGY
2. SIGMA
3. MICHIGAN
4. SPECIALIZE
5. MEDICAL
6. NOMINATED
7. NEUROSURGEON

Cipher decoded:

IF YOU WANT TO BE SOMETHING YOU HAVE TO PERCEIVE THAT SOMETHING IS POSSIBLE

222

Fern Y. Hunt
Answers

1. What college did I get my Ph. D from?
   A. New York City University
   B. New York University
   C. State University of New York
2. What year did I start working for NIST?
   A. 1978
   B. 1993
   C. 1981
3. What do I encourage students to do?
   A. medical
   B. mathematics
   C. cooking

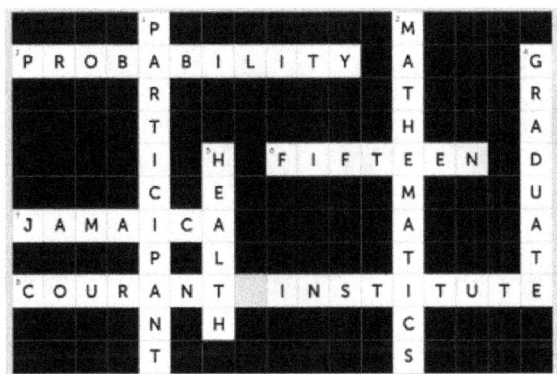

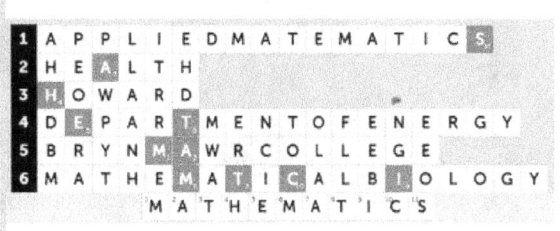

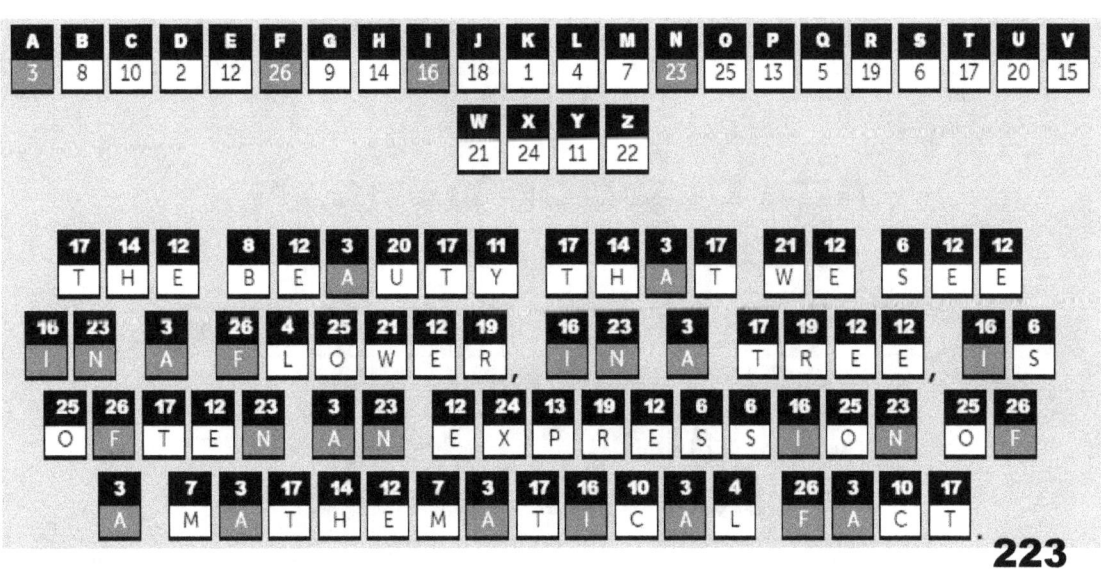

1. Which Supreme Court Justice did I clerk for?
   A. Sonia Sotomayor
   B. Clarence Thomas
   C. Stephen Breyer
2. What year did I graduate Juris Doctor cum laude?
   A. 1992
   B. 1996
   C. 1988
3. I am the first black woman to?
   A. Serve on U.S. District Court
   B. Serve on U.S. Court of Appeals
   C. Serve on U.S. Supreme Court

Ketanji Onyika Brown

Answers

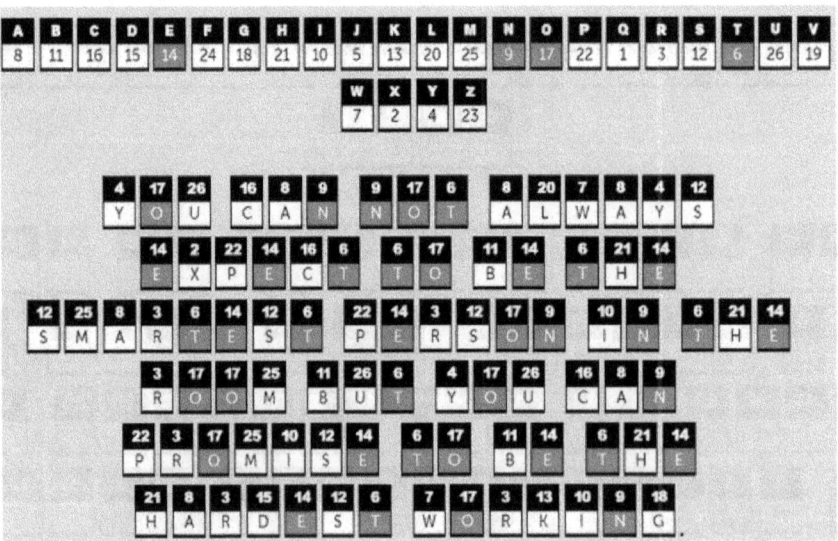

YOU CAN NOT ALWAYS EXPECT TO BE THE SMARTEST PERSON IN THE ROOM BUT YOU CAN PROMISE TO BE THE HARDEST WORKING.

1. What was the name of the college I attended?
   A. Georgia University
   B. Chattahoochee Valley Community College
   C. Georgia State University
2. What year did I become a certified Chef?
   A. 1986
   B. 1992
   C. 1991
3. I won___ gold medals at the Culinary Olympics?
   A. two
   B. one
   C. three

Darryl E. Evans

Answers

Crossword answers:
1. WORKING CHEF
2. GOLD CARROT
3. AZALEA / EXECUTIVE
4. RM
5. CHEROKEE CLUB
6. EDCAKE
7. OLYMPICS

1. COLUMBUS
2. EXECUTIVE CHEF
3. APPRENTICE
4. CULINARY OLYMPICS
5. FIVE DIAMOND
6. SOUS-CHEF
7. AZALEA RESTAURANT

ATLANTA CULINARY LANDSCAPE

A	B	C	D	E	F	G	H	I	J	K	L	M	N	O	P	Q	R	S	T	U	V
4	8	3	21	7	9	1	5	13	11	10	24	17	23	25	26	22	2	12	20	19	6

W	X	Y	Z
18	14	16	15

"TRAINING DOES NOT DO ME ANY GOOD, IF I CAN NOT PASS IT ON. SO EVERY DAY IS A TRAINING DAY FOR ME AND OTHERS."

225

1. What was my nickname for me?
   A. Lizzy
   B. Bessie
   C. Beth
2. I'm the first black woman to?
   A. earn an aviation pilot's license
   B. earn a Truck Driving license
   C. earn an Engineer's license
3. What type of pilot was I?
   A. Commercial
   B. Stunt
   C. War

Elizabeth Coleman
Answers

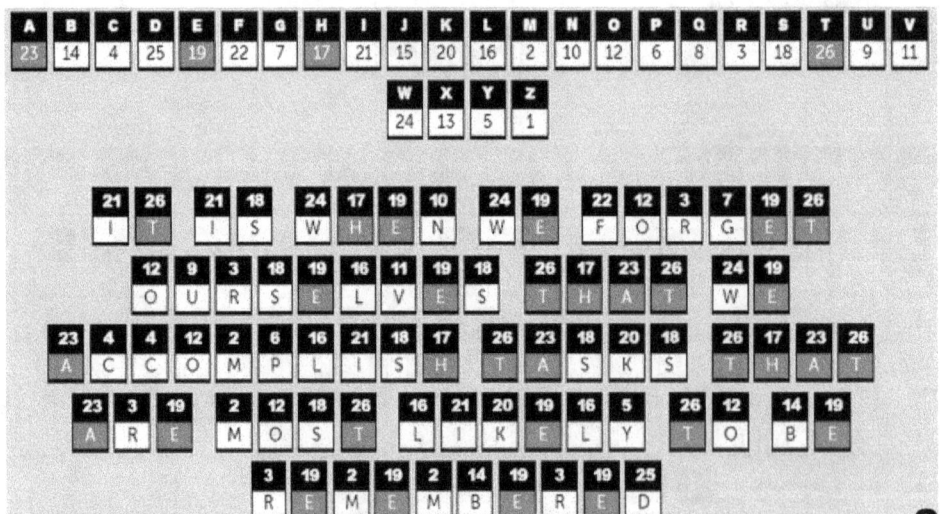

IT IS WHEN WE FORGET OURSELVES THAT WE ACCOMPLISH TASKS THAT ARE MOST LIKELY TO BE REMEMBERED.

John Wesley Cromwell
Answers

1. What college do I graduate from?
   A. Dartmouth College
   B. Colby-Sawyer College
   C. Keene State College
2. What year did I become a CPA?
   A. 1907
   B. 1923
   C. 1921
3. What did I teach when I first started teaching?
   A. English
   B. Mathematics
   C. History

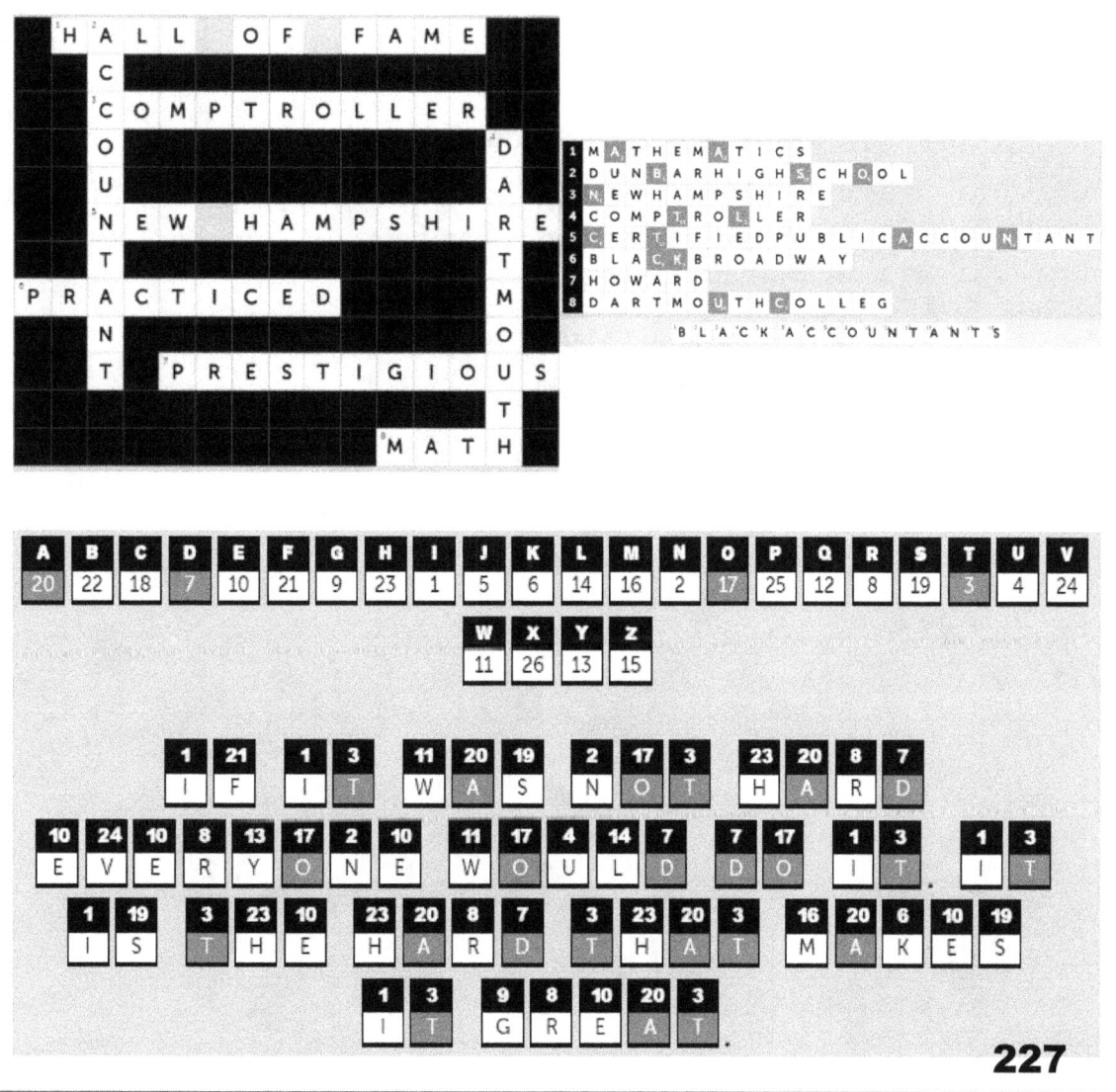

227

This book is dedicated to my grandkids
Anais Isabella Pablo-Antonio
Deyshawn Frank Chambers
Alicia Marie Jackson
Ayianna Marie Chambers
Zion Jamaris Jackson
Jayvon Jerome Jackson

ABOUT THE AUTHOR

Matthew D. Hale, the author of Black Historical Figures is a retired Marine and disabled veteran. He received his Bachelor of Arts in Computer Science from Campbell University and his Master of Science in Computer Engineering from Boston University. Matthew spends his down time making music, traveling, playing, and developing his own video games. Follow Matthew on Facebook/Meta at wegonnalearntoday, Instagram @ w_g_l_t and Tic Tok at wegonnalearntoday. Go to wegonnalearntoday.com or everydollarcountz.com for additional information.

In 2020 Matthew developed an interactive website, www.wegonnalearntoday, to provide access to Black History through games, music and videos. The website grew into the Black Historical Figures workbook series as a way to supplement the black history curricula taught in the school systems.

10 BOOK SERIES
RELEASE DATES

NOVEMBER 2022

FEBRUARY 2023

MAY 2023

AUGUST 2023

NOVEMBER 2023

GET YOUR COPY TODAY
DON'T FORGET TO TELL A FRIEND

www.ingramcontent.com/pod-product-compliance
Lightning Source LLC
Chambersburg PA
CBHW080335170426
43194CB00014B/2572